The Emergence
We Have a Communication Problem

ISBN 978-1-304-89784-8

I0427134

CHAPTERS

A collection of essays and podcast episodes elevating, rather than inhibiting, human potential and agency.

This Book, the following essays and episodes, and resources around this subject can be found at TheEmergence.io

"As iron sharpens iron, so one person sharpens another." ~~ Proverbs 27:17

Prologue

I believe in a higher power, the details of which are my own personal beliefs. I don't believe we're here through some cosmic accident but here to exercise our will through a combination of faith and exploring our own potential for the benefit of ourselves and others.

"Even the most lost soul on the street knows more than you on some things." I told this to a colleague once and I think his brain melted. But I believe this to be true. Tapping into the potential of all, from those suffering the most to the most affluent, is the foundation for a healthier society.

But with all of the increasingly advanced communication technology available at our disposal, the sharing of knowledge and resources, which one can argue is the foundation to unlock this available human potential, remains hidden behind paid and ad based silos that are funded by only the wealthiest of individuals, where access is optimized for these providers of information over the users.

The following collection of essays and podcast episodes weave a tapestry of ideas centered on reshaping communication technology to prioritize user interests and capabilities over provider-driven agendas. These reflections, spanning from the early 1960's to the inception of The Emergence.IO in October 2020, represent a journey through an evolving digital landscape. Recognizing a synergistic alignment with these ideals, I transitioned this collection to Substack, culminating in the book you are about to delve into.

My observations over the years have charted the internet's transformation from a beacon of openness and collaboration to a realm of opaqueness and control, increasingly monetized and manipulated by a few dominant forces. This shift, which I've chronicled with a growing sense of frustration, culminates in my latest essay as of the writing of this book, "We Have a Communication Problem." This piece, marking a moment of near surrender, now finds its place as a historical marker in this book – an archive for myself and, perhaps, for others who resonate with these thoughts.

As I grappled with completing this book's introduction, a pivotal announcement from Sam Altman on November 6th, 2023, regarding the OpenAI GPT store, rekindled my curiosity.

Side note: Certainly there are many very interesting Generative AI and AI companies I could call out in this intro but Open AI was the first to introduce the notion of user creators at this scale so they will be the focus of this prologue for the essays and podcast episodes that follow.

My prior engagement with ChatGPT, albeit as a casual user, hadn't fully revealed the potential of Generative AI in relation to The Emergence's core principles. However, diving deeper into Chat GPT4 and creating GPTs for the upcoming GPT store, I began to perceive a paradigm shift in communication technology – one where tools that were not reliant on deep pockets could empower user agency to create experiences for the users to explore their own interests and capabilities to ultimately harness their own potential.

This isn't to suggest that ChatGPT or similar platforms should monopolize user experiences either; such a scenario would be perilously unbalanced. Instead, it's the concept of utilizing AI to enable people to construct their queries, without the need of programming skills, that intrigues me. This process of creating, discovering, and sharing outside the confines of silos ran by shareholders resonates with the very principles that inspired The Emergence – akin to what is found in following chapters such as the pheromone trails in ant colonies or Douglas Engelbart's concept of Bootstrapping where those developing new tools for boosting Collective IQ can use what they build to enhance their own effectiveness.

Could Altman's notion of AI as a "thought partner" suggest a collaborative relationship with AI, one where our human potential is leveraged, not overshadowed. Even though Chat GPT resides inside a silo, the expression of tools created would not, which could lead to a partnership serving as a key piece in the puzzle of empowering users to tap into their potential both individually and collectively.

Then in the blink of an eye Sam Altman is fired from OpenAI who is replaced with a CEO from the media live-streaming platform Twitch, then Altman is said to move internally to Microsoft, who then moves back to Open AI as CEO, which to me lifted the veil of naivety that was beginning to settle in with a bit of blind optimism over AI.

But maybe not all is lost due to a couple of boardroom shuffles. Time will tell. But if tools are to be built to truly serve the interests of users, they need to be driven by the users and not by shareholders, and to me the only way forward is to cautiously leverage the power of AI to give people a leg up. I emphasize the word cautiously because the downside to AI controlling our perceptions is significant but should this fear keep us within the gates of the status quo? I don't believe so.

In an interview on Hard Fork two days before being removed from the Open AI board, Altman talked about his interest in keeping a version of Chat GPT available for free to the users without a reliance on ads. As you will see in Chapter 4 below, Emerging Consumer Interests Through Tunable Ads, I have a disdain for the infectious onslaught of ads in the knowledge graph. And as you will see in Chapter 7, Declaration Of Digital Independence, I believe Ben Goertzel's theory on Offer Networks through his AI company SingularityNet is an interesting alternative solution without the intermediary of money.

I ask myself frequently what would be possible if the decentralization of Blockchain could be combined with Generative AI to help create a voucher system to allow users to complete tasks to gain access to the knowledge graph for sweat equity where a working mother completes a task for someone else to receive a credit to access an AI application to better herself or to make money.

In the lens of The Emergence, the solution is to provide users with tools that are not reliant on deep pockets to empower user agency and to create experiences for the users to explore their own interests and capabilities to ultimately harness their own potential. The web and web search is not built for this. Generative AI could be a solution as long as monied interests don't swallow it whole like they did with the web.

I remain cautiously optimistic because despite these concerns, the nature of Generative AI feels fundamentally different, relying on collective learning, not popularity metrics, to potentially offer a more authentic and decentralized experience. As a self-professed curious individual, albeit not a tech expert, I see an opportunity with Generative AI helping people like myself actively participate in this new age of collective learning from the bottom up.

As I publish this book, I ponder the future direction of TheEmergence.io. Perhaps, the real purpose of this book is to inspire solutions through the lens of Generative AI, highlighting its role as a potential remedy for the communication challenges outlined throughout this book.

The question that now arises is how we, the average curious individuals, leverage these tools to solve problems – be they personal, communal, or institutional. This exploration is not about replacing programmers but leveraging their work, particularly in areas like backend development and enterprise API applications, where the potential to connect with these resources outside corporate influence seems limitless.

More specifically, what can we, the curious individuals, build with these tools to resolve problems and find solutions for ourselves and others? To leverage Generative AI to build applications from the street level rather than the boardroom level. To bring millions of creatives who would normally be shut out of building applications into the fold to solve problems and provide solutions more representative of the communities they work within.

Who will build a better tool to help identify cancer cells? A group of doctors or a medical committee tied to the bottom line of the success of an application. Who will create a better way to discover movies speaking to the interests of movie goers? A filmmaker or a movie studio tied to the bottom line selling their catalog of movies. Who will build a better way to help find resources for those suffering from mental health issues, homelessness, or substance abuse? A community activist who had suffered and overcame afflictions or an institution funded by big pharma?

Maybe an element of The Emergence will be to build potential solutions using generative AI to be a part of this new era of bottom up development unfolding before us. In service of this, I was inspired by a comment made to an X/Twitter post from Robert Scoble where he called out the ChatGPT AI hype during the GPT store announcement.

"GPTs are bait for normies - will help them realize all they can do with the bot - its just like giving ppl a coloring book vs a blank slate is all"

I replied with "get ready for the normie invasion!

According to Dictionary.com "Normie is slang for a "normal person," especially someone seen to have conventional, mainstream tastes, interests, viewpoints, etc. It is intended as an insult but often used ironically."

To sum it up, a Normie is an average person, which I believe is an unfortunate generalization and characterization, even when delivered with irony, because it is impossible to sum up the potential of a person with a generalization. We are all complex in our genetic and behavioral makeup. Whether we express this potential or not, it is a complicated matter in of itself due to the environments we live within.

But my point is, if the vast majority of the world's population are normies, then why are we not tapping into this reservoir of possibilities now that we have the ability to leverage the gears of knowledge never available to humans before? The delta of this potential is where the power lies.

This was always the idea behind The Emergence. To surface the talents of people to build better communication tech outside the influence of large corporations. But the technology wasn't available until now. ChatGPT and similar platforms, while not a panacea, act as conversation starters and roadmaps for individuals to emerge from the confines imposed by dominant corporations. If there were a path forward for The Emergence, it would be to actively participate in this conversation and to contribute, even if modestly, to this evolving solution.

And it is important to note that what follows is not an attack on big business or big government. It is an attack on the misalignment of intent with stated purpose which preys on institutions and communities both big and small. Are we here to lift people up through opportunities or hold them back through controls? When it comes to any form of communication technology, controls cloaked in opportunity do not scale well for societal progress.

I believe putting opportunity in the hands of the people; with AI, technologists, and funding sources in the background as an assist will scale better. Yes, controls over the user could still be cloaked in opportunity but when shareholders, who have no sweat equity in the game, are removed from the promise of progress, then what communication tools could be built for opportunities to reach deeper into our collective potential? Without a doubt this all goes out the window if Generative AI removes agency from the user in creating the tools and defaults back to the algorithmic monolith we see in all of our communication tools today.

AI involves significant costs due to immense requirements for computing resources, which makes it clear why substantial funding is necessary for its ongoing development. However, the central question raised is who should lead the development of the final applications. Should it be directed by the shareholders or the users?

The problem is that shareholders are going to demand a high rate of return and infinite growth which has been proven time and time again to sacrifice quality of the end solution for the user. Do we really want quantity over quality to drive Generative AI and AI in general? This is where things become concerning with this shiny new technology that even the creators struggle to comprehend.

However, when millions, if not hundreds of millions, of people begin creating solutions while sharing revenue with developers and hosting AI companies, wouldn't revenue follow? And as jobs are being displaced by automation, could AI, combined with the untapped potential of people create other sources of income while building solutions for others to benefit from? A scenario where backend developers and host AI companies continue to grow but not at the expense of the user or a better way to put it — at the expense of the people.

Add onto this potential funding from non-profit organizations, not-for-profits, government initiatives, and social impact investors, and we might begin to see a significant shift in communication technologies towards community, group, and personal-level solutions. When in the history of humankind have people had access to tools like this to leverage their own potential? Never!

Yes, we have a communication problem. Now let's let the people (the Normies) have a crack at the solution.

Chapter 1
The Emergent Web Introduction
Originally Published 11/27/18

In 1968 Douglas Engelbart hosted a groundbreaking demo to envision a future of users collaborating by text, video, and audio through networked terminals 10 years before the PC and 30 years before the birth of the web. Even though punch cards were the computer media of the day, Douglas and his team at the Stanford Research Institute were building systems to push the limits of augmenting the human connection to reimagine the confines of the written page, the TV, and the radio set, where every word articulated was an opportunity for collaboration and heightened thought.

A reimagining inspired by Vannevar Bush's seminal article As We May Think, published in the Atlantic Monthly Journal in 1945, where he laid out a future with a mesh of associative trails erecting a scaffolding of shared knowledge inspiring a young Douglas Engelbart and Ted Nelson. The latter who in addition to birthing the concept of hypertext created project Xanadu to realize the potential of these associative trails (or what he called transclusions) to liberate thought and action from conventional rules of media.

But reality rendered a different web, where connected pages evolved from Tim Berners Lee's efforts at CERN offering a more conventional yet wildly successful medium to half of the world's population (to date) to provide unprecedented access to the information of the world. Impressive indeed but did Tim Berners-Lee help build this web for people to be so easily influenced by outside forces in the exchange of information as we are seeing today?

Did he help build this web for the monetary value of the connection to supersede the personal value extracted from the medium? I think not but as noble as the cause was the effect took a turn for the worse resulting in today's noisy silos of monetized awareness. As stated in a recent Vanity Fair article, Mr. Berners Lee obviously has some regrets but apparently has not resolved himself to defeat. No...he wants to reimagine the web as it was originally intended as outlined in the World Wide Web Foundation's new Magna Carta w3.org/webat25/news/tim-berners-lee-calls-for-a-magna-carta -for-the-web-ted-talk where it is stated, "For the web to realize this potential, it must be shaped by its billions of individual users, and not by the vested interests or limited experiences of a select few. The web's ability to empower people lives with the ability of people to access, understand, and create relevant content freely and without undue interference from any company, platform, or government."

Will this time be different? How will billions of individual users claim what was once promised? How will the organizational domains of Google, Facebook, Twitter, and Apple feel about an open web where the user is in control of their own experiences? The digital revolution began with the mainframe computer finding efficiencies in organizational development evolving into the personal computer finding efficiencies in personal development.

Once connected, realms of administrative autonomy and authority, known as domains were created to help empower the user with the information of the world but over time user (personal) domains were absorbed into organizational domains wielding influence over the user as opposed to being a neutral facilitator. (Yahoo, Google, Amazon, Apple, Facebook, Twitter, Microsoft, etc.)

How could users reclaim the web? First by keeping personal domains of information created, consumed, and shared under their own authority, separate from these organizational domains and the network and the applications serving them. Where expressions and impressions of the user would be revealed based only on permissions granted and received keeping trails of activity off of the network focusing on the quality of the connection over the quantity.

At least this is Tim Berners Lee plan with his Solid framework (working with MIT) to build an open source decentralized platform of PODS Personal Online Data Stores to hold all of the information we create and consume within personal domains of our own authority where we decide what is shared and what is tracked outside the influence of organizational domains.

To build on this baseline of personal authority, Mr. Berners Lee has also launched Inrupt, a startup focused on building a development community to create application layers to interact with PODS to help build a new web of purposeful and secure interactions between users. A new web undertaken not only by Mr. Berners Lee but by a community of technologists hungry for a more resonant connection and through the lens of this writing a more emergent connection.

Mr. Berners Lee is one of many web pioneers scheduled to talk at the Douglas Engelbart 50th anniversary symposium to not only look forward but to look back to ideas passed over from mid 1940's through the early 90's where words, sentences, paragraphs, and passages would be liberated from the confines of pages and media containers to become linkable, associative, editable, and shareable based on permissions whether written, spoken, or visualized. Where visions of a new web could carry these expressions into venues for collaboration, discovery, and rediscovery regardless of login.

Back to the innovative ideas and experiments of Vannevar Bush, Douglas Engelbart, and Ted Nelson to build an associative mesh of trails to connect personal domains not through the profile but through the expressions and impressions contained within. Breaking these expressions and impressions out of the box to create opportunities to augment intelligence of the user was also at the core of Douglas Engelbart's theories on the importance of maintaining a healthy balance between human systems and tool systems to encourage a more natural flow of information rather than the artificial flow rendered today. A landscape envisioned for the user to be an active participant in crafting their own experiences rather than as a passive bystander as we see in the current iteration of the web.

In a 2007 Google talk youtube.com/watch?v=xQx-tuW9A4Q with Douglas Engelbart, a number of missed opportunities were identified that remain unresolved to this day to include Collaborative Search (17:49), Subaddressing (28:11) links inside documents, Structured Arguments (35:30), Aggregating Knowledge (44:27), Dynamic Views (48:12), and Comments in Context (51:39). Taken as a whole, the discussion provided a unique view of the largest search engine on the planet grappling with why a more expressive and emergent web had not arrived yet. A discussion taking place over 10 years ago. What technologies currently exist that speak well to these ideas?

To name a few, Feedly which allows for an open flow of information exchanged between creators and consumers through RSS feeds even as closed silos of experiences trend, Slack for harnessing individual tasks and skills into productive workflows, Cake.co (this platform no longer exists) for daring to reimagine social media as a destination for thoughtful conversations around topics, Pocket for bridging bookmarking and text to voice together, and tldrify.com to create links to highlighted passages inside web pages.

But these are the exception, not the rule. Where do we look to make these technologies the rule? We need to look beyond the technology and to the human behind the connection.

Douglas Engelbart didn't see the web as merely a connection but as a catalyst to help people build a better framework for their own understanding. His concept of bootstrapping described how technology could help augment intelligence by encouraging the user to build tools to inspire the building of tools for deeper learning. But I have read his fixation on bootstrapping divided his team at SRI where many went on to work on the PC as opposed to continuing to work on the notion of connecting users through terminals.

In hindsight, Douglas's focus on bootstrapping was for organizational development at a time when the PC promised to free users from the clutches of centralized structures which is a fear that has only increased over time. What could be learned from this bygone era to apply to a more socially aware yet skeptical environment of today where bootstrapping could focus more on personal development influencing organizational development rather than the other way around?

With a focus on providing individuals with tools to build their own framework of understanding within their own personal domains, playing a more active role in conditioning their own expressions and filtering impressions coming in. Could a demand driven from personal fulfillment encourage a supply of new technologies monetizing both personal and monetary value of the connection?

Many might wonder if this would be anathema to a web conditioned on ease of use but should the reward of understanding co-exist without effort? Universal access to information based on permissions and abilities within flexible and reasonable transaction costs, absolutely! Without effort, no! Because when the effort is taken out of the equation are we not more easily influenced?

Do we wish for a future of associative trails laid out before us by AI or by our own accord? Of course, there is a place for Artificial Intelligence but to serve, not to lead, right? At the Google talk referenced earlier, Douglas Engelbart spoke about the pushback he received in the development of his NLS system with Viewing Dynamics back in the 1960s where he was told he needed to focus on technology that was simple to use and easy to learn.

There is something to be said about working smart not working hard but how much does reward without effort inspire? When communication technology assumes inability over capability, how much of our potential is lost?

In 1999, through an experiment in self-directed learning, Sugata Mitra and colleagues placed an Internet-connected computer with programs to use into a wall near their office located in the slums of Kalkaji, New Delhi. With the screen visible to the poorest of poor walking by with absolutely no instructions to operate, children who had mostly never gazed upon a computer before crowded around the foreign object and began to click and explore.

Surprisingly, within a few hours, the children were already surfing the web. Whether the result was achieved through one child imparting basic knowledge to one another or accidental discovery of the user, the experiment proved the resiliency of the human mind to collaborate and adapt at the service of understanding. It seems industriousness serves many masters.

As methods are debated and applications created in how to connect our personal domains together for this new web, what could be done to help users build a stronger signal for understanding to emerge from a collection of individuals to help serve the whole more effectively? In Steven Johnson's book Emergence, ants sharing pheromone trails with each other for the benefit of themselves and the colony outside the centralized command of the queen ant resulted in a healthy community of ants. What is possible when we create an ecosystem of individual expressions and impressions under the authority of the individual to exchange personal value?

Where blockchain technology could create an exchange of micro and voucher transactions to more effectively align the value of our ideas, capabilities, and actions with the needs of others as well as the organizations and governments we interact with. An emergent marketplace where we could pay pennies for an exceptionally resonating paragraph behind a paywall then pay for more content as our interest dictates or trade a skill for content, a good or a service.

Where we could interact directly with a passage from pending legislation with the ability to turn on layers of context providing insight into committee sponsor benefactors, lobbyist involvement, preferred contractors, related legislation, and topic related member voting records. With access to a feedback tool to invite community members into the thread allowing legislators to identify contributors for panel discussions, creating associative trails of civic discourse.

Where every impression topic could carry a matched list of verifiable sources to consider to help prove or disprove the context of what is shared (verified through server origination, reputational authority, peer reviews, etc.) With every expression created having access to a list of sources as well. I would imagine if Facebook had this feature during the Russian hacking episode of 2016, the number of fake articles shared may have been reduced considerably.

Where a consumer discovers a product through a direct interaction with expressions related to the design, engineering, or cultural impact of the good bypassing traditional modes of marketing and advertising where influence over the transaction does not come from a third party but from the involvement of the consumer to tune out what doesn't resonate and tune in what does. Is it advertising if a good or service satisfies both an innate need and a value proposition or is it just an exchange of value? A new marketplace where associative trails of commerce emerge to reduce consumer dissonance and increase customer loyalty.

Where a comment thread in a news article allows the user to filter comments by relevance to the topic, commenter background, author and commenter quality scores, and sources cited in comments with the ability to mashup comments to share as a new associative thread serving as a new point of discovery to the article.

Where an augmented reality mirror could change the appearance of the user's face to reflect a different ethnicity, gender, or the effects of addiction with associative stories of background, struggle and strength to overcome challenges creating breadcrumbs of empathy for those different than ourselves and of the consequences in how we treat others and ourselves.

Where associative trails of learning are attached to an object of a species of tree carrying commentary from a world-renowned botanist, a local arborist, an article from an environmental journalist, and a live feed from a high school teacher discovered by a student through an immersive tag on a real tree or in a virtual world. What other objects are there to engage our minds? Could the world literally become a stage?

Where a group of sports fans separated by thousands of miles enter a virtual fantasy football game to collaborate on game stats while standing on the sidelines assigning each other roles on the coaching staff to strategize on gameplay. Each participant bringing their own skills of research, observation, and strategic thinking to the game creating associative trails of immersive interaction difficult to recreate in a non emergent world.

Do we need just another version of the web, a web 3.0, or do we need more of a reboot, where owners of personal domains create and consume information not at the pleasure of organizational domains but as a partner? Where creativity, awareness, productivity, and empathy emerge from a secure connection of expressions, not as a definition of who the user is but as a signal to what they are capable of.

A web intuitive enough for users of all ages while accessible for users regardless of background to be able to choose to read, watch, or listen to every expression made. Where every word, sentence, paragraph, or set of passages could be highlighted, bookmarked, and associated with people, places, and things through the user's own volition.

Associations, easily and openly shared based on permissions to a phone number, email, document, web page, social post, or an object in an immersive world. Associations, discoverable through advanced filtering on the user's end to paint experiences onto a canvas of understanding. Where barriers of access and cost fall as exchanges of value are revealed between users and providers uncovering potential in the most unlikely of places.

We need a better web to put the user in the driver seat of the connection because technology should not be for us to disappear into but to emerge from to become more resonant in the natural world. The purpose of this article is more question than answer as will we ever know what is best for us? Probably not. But could we challenge technologists, academics, investors, politicians, and users to find common ground in what might inspire us to be better? If there were ever something to rally around with more potential for positive change it would seem improving the human connection would be on top of the list.

As the group of notables assembles at the Computer Science Museum in Mountain View, California to celebrate the spirit of innovation and their role on building tools to inspire a better connection, maybe time could be spent looking around the room to identify future partners in the building of this new web. Looking beyond only peer groups of technologists, academics, scientists and investors but to the waitstaff, the janitorial staff, the burnt out CEO sitting nearby, the disaffected youth and the homeless person passed by in the drive in.

What is possible when the tools built are in turn tools for people to build their own better realities? Realities built through an emergent web of opportunities favoring the individual user over the influence of organizational domains where capabilities of one are aligned with the needs of another.

What could an emergent web do to empower us to do more for ourselves, each other, and the communities surrounding us? To learn more from what is done rather than what is said as well as finding solutions in disagreement. If we look deep inside you never know what we may find. Is this a Utopian pipe dream or an exercise in possibilities? I guess that would depend on the eyes of the beholder. These words are clearly written for the latter.

For those who see the possibilities in a web more responsive to the individual, it appears the time is ripe to act, evidenced by the congregation gathering to celebrate the 50th anniversary of a demo ushering in a new era of computing that has connected us but has not fully engaged us yet.

Is this an opportunity for a new round of innovation or the beginnings of a movement? Personally, I have been obsessed with the notion of technology reaching within for the last 15 years but only lately have been able to come to an understanding of what it is. Only after digging deep into the writings of Vannevar Bush with the theories and innovations of Douglas Engelbart and Ted Nelson and the arguments made in Steven Johnson's book Emergence, did I come to the realization that what I have been chasing is what is possible in an emergent connection being pushed from the efforts of the individual rather than being pulled from interactions of the masses and AI.

I do not assume the term Emergent Web will be adopted en masse but I do believe those who believe in the power of these ideas should come up with a unifying message to rally the investment community, politicians, technologists, academics, and users to see beyond only a return on investment to a return on interaction in how people are benefiting from the technologies built.

Could this new web build better tools to monitor this? Where an improvement in movement could be measured from an Alzheimer's patient interacting in a virtual world or a reduction in healthcare costs could be tracked through a tool allowing doctors to more effectively and efficiently relate patient conditions to medical coding. And most importantly, should these future technologies be allowed to fail? Thomas Edison said, "I have not failed, I've just found 10,000 ways that won't work".

True innovation only comes from repeated failures but when the bottom line of shareholders is firmly attached to an expectation of constant growth, quality seems to always suffer. Part of Douglas Engelbart's vision was to carry these innovations forward outside the bottom line into improvement communities to experiment on ideas, especially in realizing many of his ideas were unproven.

In this next incarnation of the web, what type of improvement communities or labs could be created to solicit funding from social impact investors, government subsidies, and charitable organizations to build technology to help people help themselves? Some technologies will fail, the ones that prove a benefit could be made available to an open community of apps to help existing solutions become more emergent. We have to ask ourselves, will society more likely benefit from the convenience of the masses or the deeper interactions of the individual?

Now that the technology exists to pull this off isn't the best investment to make the ones we make in ourselves. What better way to strengthen the core of this than through an emergent and purposeful connection.

Chapter 2
Reflections On The 50th anniversary Of Douglas Engelbart's
Mother Of All Demos
Originally Published: 12/6/18

Maybe the symposium wasn't the line in the sand I was
hoping for but could it have been the primer to bring the
fathers of the information age together with the future mothers
and fathers of the next evolution in communication
technology?

I recently attended the 50th anniversary of Douglas Engelbart
Mother of all Demos youtube.com/watch?v=yJDv-zdhzMY at
the Computer History Museum in Mountain View, California,
where the pioneers of the internet and the world wide web
looked back to look forward to re-imagine a web more
representative of the interests and capabilities of the user. In
attendance were Vint Cerf, Tim Berners-Lee, Ted Nelson, Tim
O'Reilly, Christina Engelbart, Brewster Kahle, Andy van Dam,
Jeff Rulifson and Alan Kay via telepresence to name a few. A
veritable who's who responsible for ringing in the dawn of the
internet age unpacking lessons learned and opportunities
missed to help decode what went wrong on the path to an
open and resonate web.

The reason I flew in from Phoenix to attend this symposium
was my feeling this meeting of the minds could serve as a line
drawn in the sand to usher in a new era of a connection more
representative of the people than only for the people. Even
though I truly enjoyed the event I came away missing a sense
of a narrative on the path forward which is more a reflection
on the current dissonance in the marketplace of ideas than
any one symposium to answer. Personally the standouts to
me were Tim Berners Lee's Solid Framework solid.mit.edu to

decentralize the web and Dan Whaley's web.hypothes.is to highlight and annotate the web but taken as a whole through no fault of their own, the symposium seemed to highlight the gap between the theories and the current state of development honoring these theories.

To be fair Christina mentioned there was another conference planned a few days after the symposium to look at future applications of Douglas Engelbart's ideas but based on the level of talent in the room, I wonder if there may have been an opportunity lost to solidify more of a message to rally users and providers in the technology, academic, and scientific communities as well as civic institutions around funding, experimentation, and building with today's palette of technology to influence a more personal web. A potential story arc to rally the troops of the young and old to get to work on building a better web to not only improve a bottom-line but what will inspire users to work better to move the line.

It is my sincerest desire to not take these words as a form of complaint for the incredible symposium presented by Christina Engelbart and her team at the Engelbart Institute but might serve as food for thought as she and others continue to work toward moving beyond theories to building technologies where the user is no longer merely an asset for the connection but an asset to themselves. To build environments where user capabilities emerge from the connection into a decentralized web of secure interactions. Interactions where the user is in control of the experiences they create and consume while challenged to become more creative, aware, productive, and empathetic in the exchange. A connection fed from the bottom up rather than from the top down.

Tim Berners Lee seems to be on this track with his Solid Framework and inrupt.com startup. web.hypothes.is seems to be in the fight. dynamicland.org looks very interesting. But as I looked through the source material on the other demos, many were clearly struggling to find funding or an audience. Maybe the symposium wasn't the line in the sand I was hoping for but it might have been the primer to bring the fathers of the information age together with the future mothers and fathers of the next evolution in communication technology?

After talking to a number of energized young women and men at the symposium, I walked away with a sense of wonder on the possibilities of a new era of theorists and technologists working side by side with those who carried the water to build a future built upon individual interests and capabilities more than commercial ones. What could be accomplished in an arguably more inclusive landscape to marry a contemporary toolset and mindset with ideas from the past to balance out the pull of artificial intelligence with the push of augmenting our own intelligence?

What is possible when we hand the wheel over to the user to more effectively collaborate and contribute to the experiences they create and consume? To be more of a participant than observer. To empower reason over reaction. To inspire deeper and more thoughtful interactions.

To some this might seem like either an impossible task or an unnecessary use of resources. To this I say do we really think a pop up laden, ad heavy, centralized collection of silos to track our behaviors to feed us relevancy is something that will scale to the favor of the user? Some will find comfort in the warm blanket of the status quo but there are others who will not. For this latter group, will the Mother of all Demos 50th anniversary symposium will be the spark to light this fire? Maybe not but could it be the kindling?

Chapter 3
Emergent Representation Of The People
Originally Published 1/13/19

In a representative democracy, we vote for elected officials to represent our interests through the policies they put forth but is our influence not stifled when we build more of a relationship with the legislator over that of the legislation drafted? It seems to reason a representative government would be better served when the represented are more aware of what is being codified than what is only being promised. And wouldn't the representative be better served when they are better able to tune in to feedback from their constituency as it directly relates to what is being written rather than from random comment threads, emails, or through the coaxing of a talking head from a media outlet?

At the outset, it seems like the vast majority of the electorate would never bother with the sausage making of governing but what if a personal connection was made between the legislation and the constituent? Would the represented be more inclined to share their voice if they were notified of a passage in a piece of legislation impacting their commute to work, an increase in their local taxes, or a new provision to increase access to community services?

Would the electorate dig deeper if they were able to clearly see the breadcrumbs of influence between committee members, lobbyists, committee member benefactors, and contractors involved with topics within the pending legislation? Would they be encouraged to engage more when their feedback is voted up based on the relevance and resourcefulness of their interactions or cited as a contributor to the passage in the legislation when enacted? Could these tools ultimately provide valuable feedback to the legislators and provide a unique perspective to the electorate on the intricacies of the legislative process to decrease the dissonance between the representative and the represented?

What is possible when the electorate emerges from the sidelines of government into a true representational force? Would they be less tolerant of keeping those in office who act in legislating differently than the way in which they speak? This may seem like an impossible task in a gridlocked government with an information overloaded electorate but the technology already exists to provide context to legislation and tools are coming online to annotate and enable collaboration on existing pages.

Where enterprises such as the Sunlight Foundation https://sunlightfoundation.com, GovTrack.us, OpenSecrets.org, and Web.Hypothes.is could begin to break down the barriers of closed governance and top-down innovation to encourage people to become more participant than adherent.

We have to ask ourselves, would the government be a better representation of the people when people are more involved with what is written than only what is said? Yes, people en masse are not specialists in any given topic but the same goes for our legislators who rely on the voice of industry professionals and lobbyists to help inform what is drafted which can carry an agenda outside the interests of the public? But what about tapping into the specialties, vocations, and interests of the public to align their experiences and perspective with what is drafted to help move the public from a passive voice to an active resource?

A government with an ear on the tracks of public discourse could be a powerful force when thoughtful and productive interactions surface between the representative and the represented. Imagine the possibilities when a high school student engages with a legislator around a specific detail on a piece of legislation their recent studies illuminated. Or to hear from a scientist's findings on a draft item bypassing traditional means of legislative discovery. Where insightful comments and profiles could be bookmarked to passages of working legislation for consideration as it makes its way through the congressional record.

What is possible when elected officials and the electorate are more finely tuned around what is drafted to regulate, authorize, outlaw, fund, sanction, grant, declare, or restrict? It is believed here a more representative form of government will emerge to help express the will of the people more effectively. How could this happen? Through the eventual mass adoption of technologies to fold public discourse into civic understanding to build a stronger bridge between the governing and the governed. A future only possible when the tools are funded and able to demonstrate to investors and the public not only how often but how effectively the tools are used to the benefit of both the legislators and the public.

The purpose of this article is to engage influencers in both technology and government around ideas to help build a future more representative of the people. Using technology to attach and filter public comments to legislation through a layer of context is not a panacea for perfect governance but it could be a means to help keep our unalienable rights in check. If you feel this is important, please feel free to share comments, ideas, or resources here to help incorporate these ideas into the reality of governing.

Chapter 4
Emerging Consumer Interests Through Tunable Ads
Originally Published 3/5/19

I've been saying for years it's not advertising if we're interested, holding onto the promise of technology one day delivering on my wishful thinking. But here we are in 2019 with 3.2 billion users connected online through PC's, laptops, tablets, smartphones, and smartwatches where ads influence our decisions whether by mirroring our behaviors or algorithmically choosing for us. Either way not only is there a disconnect between the advertiser and consumer interests but there is also a growing sense of manipulation and distraction.

Everywhere we look online, ad servers are tuning our behaviors and interests to a bottom line not attached to the consumer. The argument here is what is possible if ad servers were tuned to the interests of the consumer to be drivers and not only passengers in the discovery of goods and services? Ad networks subsidize the distribution of content through ads mixed in with native content marked as sponsored, delivered through algorithmic triggers from rules set by the host site, visitor IP addresses, and cookies collected.

 The idea behind Tunable Ads would be to allow consumers and advertisers to adjust ads, wherever found, in a personal and permission-based ad profile. The advertisers would select criteria to best represent the features and benefits of the offering while the consumer would rank criteria to serve ads better speaking to their interests.

Why doesn't this already exist? I believe a primary reason is the current state of a top-down, centralized web monetizing behaviors outside of consumer control creates a marketplace driven more by advertiser influence rather than consumer interests. When the current model is printing money, where is the incentive to change? But the father of the World Wide Web, Tim Berners Lee through his new startup Inrupt is looking to rewrite the rules of a centralized web by moving control back to users through Personal Online Data Stores (PODS) within a decentralized framework.

Where the centralized web collects user data through cookies and form fills on the network accessible to the highest bidder, a decentralized connection of PODS would allow the user to store personal information and web history in a personal cloud to help secure and personalize web experiences.

What is possible when a personalized and permission-based framework allows the consumer to set conditions on how they would like to engage with products and services as opposed to only how a publisher or advertiser would? I believe an increase in consumer engagement and a decrease in consumer dissonance would result, not only providing new pathways for a healthier exchange but open up new opportunities for economically disadvantaged groups to access information and services.

To be clear, I do not work for Inrupt nor do I have an association with their organization but I do have a great deal of respect for what Tim Berners-Lee is looking to accomplish and had the great pleasure of meeting him at a Douglas Engelbart conference recently. Even though I've had thoughts of Tunable Ads for many years it was only until I learned about his work on the Solid Framework at MIT and his startup Inrupt with John Bruce that I felt an environment might be built to actually pull something like this off.

What would a Tunable Ad network look like using a decentralized framework? In my view, as opposed to an ad server only collecting information from consumer behavior and contextual triggers, the ad server would access information from the efforts of the consumer collected through surveys accessible by the ad servers through permissions granted. But what about the supply side?

If Tim Berners Lee's PODS could be a tool to help consumers leverage their own data could it be used to help advertisers leverage theirs? Could an expanded palette of descriptive criteria through an advertiser survey better align their offerings with the interests of the consumer? To help better relate the nuances of their offering to an increasingly sophisticated consumer? To help build a more resonant and direct connection with their market?

I spoke with Michael Nevins, Chief Marketing Officer for SmartAdServer.com, who in an article

mediapost.com/publications/article/315609/publishers-path-le ads-to-private-garden.html

on Media post, spoke of the importance of building publisher private gardens rather than only walled gardens of social and search. In the article he offered, "Finally, with the emergence of credible, open and data-protective tech platforms in 2018, publishers can now wean themselves off their disproportionate reliances on walled gardens and, in effect, nurture their own private gardens. " He added, "The result would be greater user lifetime revenue and audience loyalty within a safe, premium content ecosystem, often missing in the typical programmatic setting."

When advertisers are looking to build audience loyalty wouldn't trust become a key ingredient? A trust eroding since web 2.0 began to build AI driven walled gardens. But here we are at the doorstep of a new web. A new decentralized web that will only become a reality off of the backs of innovative use cases. I can't imagine a better use case than the controlled environment of an advertising ecosystem.

Below, I have conceptualized this by mocking up consumer and advertiser surveys to collect interests from consumers and features/benefits from advertisers. Within a POD framework, I imagine the surveys could be housed by a third party app pushing and pulling data from encrypted PODS serving as a secure carrier between ad servers, consumers, and advertisers where relevance could be delivered not only from Ad Servers and AI but from the efforts of the users.

Is it wishful thinking for users to put in the effort to yield better ads on both sides of the equation? It depends on the 3rd party application. If entertainment can be gamified, why can't our interests? How could a UI motivate the advertiser to annotate their offerings to resonate with the consumer? How could a UI motivate the consumer to filter these annotations to relate offerings to their core interests and situations where AI helps but does not lead? What could be built within a decentralized connection to supplement inferred data with expressive data to help build a more resonant exchange between people and providers?

The surveys below and the purpose of this essay is to exercise the possibilities of emerging interests of the consumer through Tunable Ads? In the following examples, the surveys would be marked as private by default with the ability for the user to grant permission for ad servers to access data from the surveys by request. The quality of the ads could be rated by the consumer and the performance of the ads could be rated by the advertiser to help increase the quality of the exchange. Interests could be ordered by dragging topics and subtopics to the top or bottom. The list order, date, and frequency of changes could be used to program ads delivered to the consumer on participating websites.

The image below is how I see the concept folding into a site featuring Tunable Ads through a fictional interface called ADTUNE.

Once the visitor accesses the ADTUNE app they would be delivered to the surveys described below through a 3rd party app pulling data from consumer and advertiser PODS. The app would serve as a gateway for both the consumer and the advertiser to manage their experiences on the ad network. For the consumer, could the gateway be a means to blend and bookmark interesting ad content with native content to reduce the distractive forces of non relevant ads? For the advertiser, could it be a means to increase reach to interested consumers?

Would an increase in engagement on both sides of the exchange translate into an optimized revenue model for the host as well? All difficult questions to answer without testing these ideas against a traditional ad delivery model begging the question why wouldn't we want to know? As new technologies become more immersive where experiences begin to surround us it is easy to imagine a future of amplified influence. Is it better for society for this influence to fall to the favor of the consumers or the advertisers? The users or the providers? Or is it better to move toward a healthy balance between the two? We now have the tools to pull this off but do we have the will?

What is proposed here is to create a pilot program to test these theories in the controlled environment of the Solid Framework in its infancy to see how user control over programmatic controls might scale in a decentralized connection.

To carry this program forward I am looking to identify a social impact investor, a development team within a University, an ad server firm, and a user group to collaborate on this project to build the 3rd party app as described within. In the end, are we all not consumers of goods, services, and experiences? What could be gained in exploring the potential of communities and a marketplace driven by the consumer within a private and secure exchange? I believe more than we can imagine.

The topics and subtopics in the surveys presented below are only primers to start a conversation around the viability of aligning the interests of consumers and advertisers through Tunable Ads. What could be built to gamify this exchange? To inspire engagement?

Tunable Ad User Survey

Drag topics and subtopics to the top to rank your interests.

LIFESTYLE

Adventure

Competition

Thrill

Work

Professional

Leisure

Family

FAVORITE COLOR

Blue

Brown

White

Purple

etc.

VALUE

Convenience

Luxury

Bargain

SECTOR

Technology

Consumer

Robotics

Music

Science

Investments

Insurance

Health

Religion

Politics

Travel

Movies

Food

Transportation

Car

Rideshare

Motorcycle

Airline

Train

Books

Tunable Ad Advertiser Survey

Choose the interests below to best describe your offering.

LIFESTYLE

Adventure

Competition

Thrill

Work

Professional

Leisure

Family

COLOR

Blue

Brown

White

Purple

VALUE

Convenience

Luxury

Bargain

SECTOR

Technology

Consumer

Robotics

Music

Science

Investments

Insurance

Health

Religion

Politics

Travel

Movies

Food

Transportation

Car

Rideshare

Motorcycle

Airline

Train

Books

Chapter 5
Why Tim Berners Lee's Decentralized Web (Inrupt) Is
important
Originally Published 4/17/19

In the forward (1946) to a new print of Aldous Huxley's 1931
opus A Brave New World, Aldous wrote. "Only a large-scale
popular movement toward decentralization and self-help can
arrest the present tendency toward statism. At present, there
is no sign that such a movement will take place".

Whether it is believed we are headed to the dystopian future
illustrated in A Brave New World or not, I believe it could be
argued we are headed toward a form of statism over our
experiences. Statism as defined is "a political system in which
the state has substantial centralized control over social and
economic affairs". Maybe political systems within democratic
nations have remained relatively safe but it appears a system
in which the web has substantial centralized control over
social and economic affairs is seemingly creeping into reality.

Imagine living in a world without technology and one day a
switch was turned on for public and private entities to listen to
what you say and hear, watch what you see and read, and
monitor where you go. Now imagine if the information
collected was used to filter what you see and hear to influence
the decisions you make and the actions you take? Would this
be OK?

I would imagine not but this is the web as we know it today. A
reality introduced, not at the flip of a switch, but slowly over
time luring users through the carrot of convenience over
clarity of thought. A connection of experiences depositing
primal needs, desires, and frustrations of users into a

centralized repository optimized to the bottom line of the provider over the user. At least this is what appears to be rising to the surface of a centralized web.

What makes the web different from other information systems of the telephone, TV, or radio? On the web, we are increasingly connected to both each other and centralized providers like no other time in history, exposing our collective intelligence to the threats of mass influence. Some may argue this could lead to oppression of our will but at the least I believe it is leading to a repression of our potential.

When we engage with content on the web or through apps, we are providing data points representative of our lives lived to those not invited to the party. What if these data points were under the control of our own personal domain rather than the centralized authority of ISPs (AT&T, Comcast, Verizon), edge providers (Google, Facebook, Apple, Amazon), advertising networks/servers (Doubleclick, OpenX), and browsers (Chrome, IE, Safari)? What if we were given the tools to render relevance and context on our own terms? To be more participant than a passenger in building better relationships with other users, products, services, and information?

This is the plan from the founder of the World Wide Web, Tim Berners Lee and the team at the startup Inrupt to re-imagine the web as a decentralized connection between users to build better bridges between personal domains. Personal domains controlled through Personal Online Data Stores (PODS) evolving from Mr. Berners Lee's work on the Solid framework at MIT. Why is this important? Because the web is becoming too powerful of a force in the human experience to be controlled by handfuls of ISP's, edge providers, advertising networks, and browsers.

If a few social networks were able to disrupt a presidential election, what is down the road when our cars, refrigerators, eyeglasses, or even our thoughts are connected? Do we want a future powered by a centralized web feeding at the trough of big public data to influence consumer behavior? Or do we want a future powered by a decentralized web empowering consumer behavior through a private connection to take back the reins of our own experiences?

Where do the opportunities lie in building off a decentralized, personalized, and private framework? Inrupt is looking to find out by inviting a community of developers and innovators to build applications to securely move personal data into and out of Solid PODS to help provide agency over user experiences. Isn't it time we had the toolset to gain control over our interactions with media companies, organizations, or even our government?

We now have the opportunity to move the user to the front seat of the exchange through a decentralized connection. A new reality, important not only for the user, but the communities they engage with. History has much to tell about extremes rendered through communities under centralized control. Now is the time to rethink the web of the future so we don't repeat the mistakes of our past.

I write on the intersection of technology and human interests and do not have an affiliation with Inrupt.

Learn more about Inrupt and the Solid Framework.
inrupt.com

solid.mit.edu

github.com/solid

twitter.com/inrupt

Chapter 6
Are We Losing The Web To Shareholder Influence?
Originally Published 6/23/19

I ran across an interesting article, DHS to Move Biometric
Data on Hundreds of Millions of People to Amazon Cloud,

nextgov.com/modernization/2019/06/dhs-move-biometric-data
-hundreds-millions-people-amazon-cloud/157837/

discussing Amazon's cloud leveraging our biometric data but
as 25,000 Amazon employees

usatoday.com/story/money/nation-now/2018/11/13/amazon-hq
-2-split-new-york-city-crystal-city-virginia/1985969002

move next door to the Pentagon, one has to wonder what
path we may be taken down. Of course, there will be firewalls,
redundancies, and standards met but think about how many
of our experiences are being captured under the domains of
massive corporations (Amazon, Google, Facebook, Twitter,
Apple, Microsoft) as well as governmental entities
(Department of Homeland Security and the NSA). Now think
about who owns the rights to these captured experiences? Do
We?

The rights to our bio-metric data. Our words. Our sleeping
patterns. Our heart rate. Where we are going. What we are
doing. What is in our refrigerator? What we are interested in?

Are we in control of our own experiences on the web? Is the
promise of the open and flourishing web of the 90s slipping
through our fingers to the influence of massive corporate
domains beholden to shareholder expectations of growth?

How concerned should we be about this intake of our experiences into vast monetized silos outputting influence onto what we read, hear, and watch? If we're not worried, I hazard to guess we are not paying attention, we don't care, or we believe there's nothing we can do about it.

Is this a grand Orwellian plot for mind control or a continuous series of subtle nudges to condition our experiences to maximize a bottom line attached to shareholder value and political expediency? I go for the latter but at the very least the evolution of the World Wide Web has become a centralized repository to extract more value from the user than for the user. And this is a missed opportunity of epic proportions as the fundamentals of the web to positively impact society are in place.

Certainly, we are connected like no other time in history with the mobility to consume and share experiences with each other regardless of time and location. Where advancements in artificial intelligence are beginning to provide context to what we can and cannot see. Where robots will begin to lighten our load and sensors will begin to extend our awareness. And where immersive technologies will soon begin to render amazing new worlds onto our existing realities. All opportunities waiting for us to take advantage of but when we are not in control, how will we ever not be the ones taken advantage of? How can we claim control over the technology being built in the name of our interests? Three examples of innovative ideas on the scene today come to mind to lead the way.

Focus on legislation to establish user data rights
Europe's GDPR

en.m.wikipedia.org/wiki/General_Data_Protection_Regulation

Decentralize and contextualize the web
Tim Berners Lee and the startup Inrupt (Personal Online Data Stores, Separating User Data from Applications, The Semantic Web) inrupt.com

Decentralize Artificial Intelligence
Singularitynet.IO (Distributed AI development, Offer Networks, Blockchain)

What could be done to build a more private, secure, and resonant web where the user retains control of experiences created and consumed? Where we are inspired to create, collaborate, and contribute more than we are merely entertained or provoked. Where we lead more than we are led. Where stakeholders are more influential than shareholders elevating purpose over profit only. The future of the web and societal progress is in our hands and our minds. What are We going to do about it?

Chapter 7
Declaration Of Digital Independence
Originally Published 7/19/19

I have been following Larry Sanger, who is the co-founder of Wikipedia, and see he just posted a Declaration of Digital Independence on his blog with a petition to sign on Change.org. I agree with every word of the Declaration and even though this seems pie in the sky, I believe there are fundamental shifts in the marketplace at hand where decentralization of the web and data privacy laws may make much of this possible. Always an optimist until the day I die!

From Larry Sanger.
larrysanger.org/2019/06/declaration-of-digital-independence

Humanity has been contemptuously used by vast digital empires. Thus it is now necessary to replace these empires with decentralized networks of independent individuals, as in the first decades of the Internet. As our participation has been voluntary, no one doubts our right to take this step. But if we are to persuade as many people as possible to join together and make reformed networks possible, we should declare our reasons for wanting to replace the old.

We declare that we have unalienable digital rights, rights that define how information that we individually own may or may not be treated by others, and that among these rights are free speech, privacy, and security. Since the proprietary, centralized architecture of the Internet at present has induced most of us to abandon these rights, however reluctantly or cynically, we ought to demand a new system that respects them properly. The difficulty and divisiveness of wholesale reform means that this task is not to be undertaken lightly. For years we have approved of and even celebrated enterprise as it has profited from our communication and labor without compensation to us. But it has become abundantly clear more recently that a callous, secretive, controlling, and exploitative animus guides the centralized networks of the Internet and the corporations behind them.

The long train of abuses we have suffered makes it our right, even our duty, to replace the old networks. To show what train of abuses we have suffered at the hands of these giant corporations, let these facts be submitted to a candid world.

They have practiced in-house moderation in keeping with their executives' notions of what will maximize profit, rather than allowing moderation to be performed more democratically and by random members of the community.

They have banned, shadow-banned, throttled, and demonetized both users and content based on political considerations, exercising their enormous corporate power to influence elections globally.

They have adopted algorithms for user feeds that highlight the most controversial content, making civic discussion more emotional and irrational and making it possible for foreign powers to exercise an unmerited influence on elections globally.

They have required agreement to terms of service that are impossible for ordinary users to understand, and which are objectionably vague in ways that permit them to legally defend their exploitative practices.

They have marketed private data to advertisers in ways that no one would specifically assent to.

They have failed to provide clear ways to opt out of such marketing schemes.

They have subjected users to such terms and surveillance even when users pay them for products and services.

They have data-mined user content and behavior in sophisticated and disturbing ways, learning sometimes more about their users than their users know about themselves; they have profited from this hidden but personal information.

They have avoided using strong, end-to-end encryption when users have a right to expect total privacy, in order to retain access to user data.

They have amassed stunning quantities of user data while failing to follow sound information security practices, such as encryption; they have inadvertently or deliberately opened that data to both illegal attacks and government surveillance.

They have unfairly blocked accounts, posts, and means of funding on political or religious grounds, preferring the loyalty of some users over others.

They have sometimes been too ready to cooperate with despotic governments that both control information and surveil their people.

They have failed to provide adequate and desirable options that users may use to guide their own experience of their services, preferring to manipulate users for profit.

They have failed to provide users adequate tools for searching their own content, forcing users rather to employ interfaces insultingly inadequate for the purpose.

They have exploited users and volunteers who freely contribute data to their sites, by making such data available to others only via paid application program interfaces and privacy-violating terms of service, failing to make such freely-contributed data free and open source, and disallowing users to anonymize their data and opt out easily.

They have failed to provide adequate tools, and sometimes any tools, to export user data in a common data standard.

They have created artificial silos for their own profit; they have failed to provide means to incorporate similar content, served from elsewhere, as part of their interface, forcing users to stay within their networks and cutting them off from family, friends, and associates who use other networks.

They have profited from the content and activity of users, often without sharing any of these profits with the users.

They have treated users arrogantly as a fungible resource to be exploited and controlled rather than being treated respectfully, as free, independent, and diverse partners.

We have begged and pleaded, complained, and resorted to the law. The executives of the corporations must be familiar with these common complaints; but they acknowledge them publicly only rarely and grudgingly. The ill treatment continues, showing that most of such executives are not fit stewards of the public trust.

The most reliable guarantee of our privacy, security, and free speech is not in the form of any enterprise, organization, or government, but instead in the free agreement among free individuals to use common standards and protocols. The vast power wielded by social networks of the early 21st century, putting our digital rights in serious jeopardy, demonstrates that we must engineer new—but old-fashioned—decentralized networks that make such clearly dangerous concentrations of power impossible.

Therefore, we declare our support of the following principles.

Principles of Decentralized Social Networks

We free individuals should be able to publish our data freely, without having to answer to any corporation.We declare that we legally own our own data; we possess both legal and moral rights to control our own data.Posts that appear on social networks should be able to be served, like email and blogs, from many independent services that we individually control, rather than from databases that corporations exclusively control or from any central repository.

Just as no one has the right to eavesdrop on private conversations in homes without extraordinarily good reasons, so also the privacy rights of users must be preserved against criminal, corporate, and governmental monitoring; therefore, for private content, the protocols must support strong, end-to-end encryption and other good privacy practices. As is the case with the Internet domain name system, lists of available user feeds should be restricted by technical standards and protocols only, never according to user identity or content.

Social media applications should make available data input by the user, at the user's sole discretion, to be distributed by all other publishers according to common, global standards and protocols, just as are email and blogs, with no publisher being privileged by the network above another. Applications with idiosyncratic standards violate their users' digital rights.

Accordingly, social media applications should aggregate posts from multiple, independent data sources as determined by the user, and in an order determined by the user's preferences. No corporation, or small group of corporations, should control the standards and protocols of decentralized networks, nor should there be a single brand, owner, proprietary software, or Internet location associated with them, as that would constitute centralization.

Users should expect to be able to participate in the new networks, and to enjoy the rights above enumerated, without special technical skills. They should have very easy-to-use control over privacy, both fine- and coarse-grained, with the most private messages encrypted automatically, and using tools for controlling feeds and search results that are easy for non-technical people to use.

We hold that to embrace these principles is to return to the sounder and better practices of the earlier Internet and which were, after all, the foundation for the brilliant rise of the Internet. Anyone who opposes these principles opposes the Internet itself. Thus we pledge to code, design, and participate in newer and better networks that follow these principles, and to eschew the older, controlling, and soon to be outmoded networks.

We, therefore, the undersigned people of the Internet, do solemnly publish and declare that we will do all we can to create decentralized social networks; that as many of us as possible should distribute, discuss, and sign their names to this document; that we endorse the preceding statement of principles of decentralization; that we will judge social media companies by these principles; that we will demonstrate our solidarity to the cause by abandoning abusive networks if necessary; and that we, both users and developers, will advance the cause of a more decentralized Internet.

Please sign if you agree!

You can also sign on Change.org.

change.org/p/social-media-executives-decentralize-social-media-a-declaration-of-digital-independence

Chapter 8
Free Market Parity Through Decentralization
Originally Published 9/27/19

The following quotes illustrate foundational ideas and warnings for a free market to flourish which I believe have been lost in what has been rendered, especially through the lens of the evolution of the web to date as a centralized force beholden to shareholder growth over stakeholder interests.

"They say nothing concerning the bad effects of high profits. They are silent in regards to the pernicious effects of their own gains. They complain of only those of other people"
—Adam Smith, The Wealth of Nations.

"How many people ruin themselves by laying out money on trinkets of frivolous utility? What pleases these lovers of toys is not so much the utility, as the aptness of the machines which are fitted to promote it."
— Adam Smith, The Theory of Moral Sentiments

"Labour, therefore, is the real measure of the exchangeable value of all commodities. The real price of everything, what everything really costs to the man who wants to acquire it, is the toil and trouble of acquiring it."
— Adam Smith, The Wealth of Nations

It is important to note the mission of this essay is not to devalue the importance of the shareholder or corporations in the market but to call out the evolution of the free market away from core principles tied to the productive exchange of labor to a reliance on shareholder growth we see today. Where the stock price of a good or service has become more important than the efforts and interests of the stakeholders (workers/consumers) involved. A reality more reflective of a game of roulette than a plan for a representative market, better at keeping a few freighters afloat than lifting most boats.

All shareholders are stakeholders and some stakeholders are shareholders so the quest for balance is either within us or among us. Either way, the lack of parity between the two fails the tenets of capitalism's promise of enlightened self-interest in a mutually beneficial environment for trade. A reality bearing down on an exchange of value attached to a perpetually moving bottom line chasing quantity sold at the expense of quality delivered or raising the threshold of quality outside the reach of the average stakeholder.

In a free market, McDonald's stakeholders have a right to eat or make an endless supply of big macs and shareholders have the right to profit from it. Just as shareholders have a right to profit from stakeholder's insulin shots, their college degrees, or the information they consume but at what point does the pendulum swing too far to shareholder interests where the health of the market is sacrificed? Where the lifeblood of a free market, the enlightenment of self-interest, are either priced out of the market or under-served by the quality of it.

In the mid-90s, the birth of the World Wide Web was the great hope to bring stakeholders into parity with shareholders through the power of choice but Web 2.0 arrived and corralled stakeholders into silos of corporate influence widening the gap instead of narrowing it. A gap fueled by a top-down exchange feeding off an increasingly non-productive exchange of labor rapidly moving stakeholders through information rather than into it where the potential of labor erodes not only from the distractive forces of the web but also through the replacement of labor through automation. It seems the lever of technology through market forces appears to be more of a facilitator to benefit provider influence than a catalyst for users to benefit from the spoils of their labor. We have to ask ourselves if we are in a free market or an influenced market? The argument here is that we are in the latter.

What then is the best course of action to achieve parity between the stakeholder and the shareholder toward a more representative free market? In my mind, it is not through fiat or redistribution of wealth but through the distribution of opportunity to enlighten self-interest in a mutually beneficial environment for trade. And It so happens we have the best mutually beneficial environment at our disposal, connecting over 80% of the developed world's producers and consumers.

But the problem is the world wide web has been co-opted by commercial pursuits influencing self-interests more than manifesting self-interests from user's agency. Where a lack of user/stakeholder control over their own experiences tamps down the broad spectrum of human ingenuity available within a free market of ideas, especially in a connected one.

What is possible when the stakeholder retains control over the experiences they consume and what they produce? When they have agency over what they find rather than what Facebook, Twitter, Google, or Apple finds for them. When they are in control, connected, and not distracted, what could stakeholders find or produce at work, at play, in competition, in their community, in their government, or in their relationships to drive better realities forward? To cross-pollinate value derived from their efforts regardless of their station in life to bring more human capabilities to a market rapidly being outsourced by automation.

As the web continues to become the gateway to the market through an endless collection of public websites, productivity apps, social silos, corporate intranets, sensor data, and e-commerce transactions, an opportunity exists to elevate the role of the stakeholder to bring back foundational ideas of labor driving the free market. Not through the centralized, top-heavy web, we see today influencing engagement but through a decentralized connection inspiring influence to emerge from a user base of stakeholders in technology, business, community, civics and the market in general.

A connection strengthened by user inquiry, collaboration, and context to push the market forward in the interests of the connected rather than the connecting. What would a decentralized connection look like? Many potential solutions are arriving on the scene today but there is one legislative framework and three foundational technological frameworks I believe speak well to moving stakeholders away from an influenced market to a free and influential market through decentralization.

A Bill of Data Rights
This might be the most important of the four as technology frameworks are a combination of 1s and 0s but the information created and consumed is at the core of the human experience. When humans do not own their experiences, how influential could they ever really be? The EU's General Data Protection Regulation (GDPR) is looking to answer this question of ownership by protecting user data rights through legislation, illuminated through the following opening passage of the GDPR, "The protection of natural persons in relation to

the processing of personal data is a fundamental right." An opening salvo establishing personal data rights as the U.S. and the rest of the world grapples with the political and economic realities of putting a genie monetizing user experiences back in the bottle.

No easy task as monetizing user experiences are at the very core of Big Tech's business model and part and parcel of their continued push to influence consumer demand. Big tech may be a small slice of the entire market but now that data is the most valuable asset in the world, with a handful of companies effectively controlling the flow of consumer data, the stakeholder is becoming less influential in the market limiting the scope of human potential. But is the fix a question of data ownership or data rights?

An essay from MIT technology review titled, It's Time for a Bill of Data Rights,

medium.com/mit-technology-review/its-time-for-a-bill-of-data-rights-b2482d300095

argues data ownership "not only does not fix existing problems; it creates new ones. Instead, we need a framework that gives people rights about how their data is used without requiring them to take ownership of it themselves". Now that Facebook includes user ownership in their terms of service, we have to ask ourselves, can we trust them or any other information provider with our data? Should we ever have? But establishing universal data rights at a policy level is a difficult proposition in the absence of a technological framework to ground these rights as it is difficult to enforce rules without clear boundaries.

Three technology frameworks coming onto the scene may help establish these boundaries by grounding data rights to the will and control of the individual user. To balance the interests of stakeholders with shareholders not only through Adam Smith's division of labor but through a distribution of labor only possible through a secure and decentralized connection.

A bottom-up connection better realizing Smith's notion of an invisible hand pushing people to create, compete, and consume through the pursuit of their own self-interests to release human ingenuity into the market. Maybe the lack of a resonant connection between the exchange of producers and consumers is what has tied Adam Smith's invisible hand behind the back of social progress all along.

The Decentralized Web
This is the first of the three technological frameworks I believe will help put the genie back in the bottle by re-engineering the web as a distributed connection to secure and empower user experiences over the interests of providers. Although there are browsers (Brave), Search portals (DuckDuckGo.com), and Social sites (Minds.com) committed to protecting user data, the vast majority of web destinations continue to collect user experiences to influence user behavior or sell these experiences to third party providers.

Why would providers do otherwise when mechanisms in the market fall short of establishing and enforcing guidelines to favor the user? Why change when the public at large continues to devour experiences targeted toward their behavior over their explicit interests? If inquiry were a mouse a better mousetrap is needed to prime demand for deeper and more purposeful engagements across a wider swath of stakeholders. To empower human experiences from within and across personal domains rather than experiences only powered by corporate domains. This is the potential of the decentralized web, to securely store user experiences in a distributed and structured environment, serving as a culture in a petri dish of collective knowledge.

At the forefront of the push toward a decentralized web is the father of the world wide web, Tim Berners Lee and the startup Inrupt, built off of Mr. Berners Lee's work at MIT on the Solid Framework solidproject.org. What makes the Solid framework stand out? At the core of the technology is the protection of the user experience through Personal Online Datastores (PODS) separating data produced, consumed, and shared by the user from the applications accessing the data (Social Media, Search, Browsers, Smartphone apps, etc.).

A framework providing access to personal vaults or series of vaults protecting user data rights and their self-interests from the influence of outside forces. What is the point of enforcing user data rights at a policy level without a means to secure these rights at a system level? But the Solid framework is less a system of control than a standard to build off of providing developers an open environment using principles of structured data and the semantic web to move control over to the users.

What is possible when the user gains trust in the information they create, consume, and share? When they can manifest experiences to serve themselves and their communities better within a marketplace of education, healthcare, technology, entertainment, government, and social welfare? When a student can store their interests and situations in a secure environment (Solid PODS) to tune curriculum found in a learner application to help increase a thirst for the encountered subject.

When someone facing a mental crisis could immediately match and securely connect their situation, insurance coverage, and billing information with the secure profile of a counselor with similar attributes bypassing the institutional trappings of a centralized approach to mental health. A couple of examples serving as only a glimpse of what is possible in an encrypted intentional exchange backed up by a "Bill of Data Rights".

If the decentralized web were to be a trusted canvas to lay experiences on, what are the motivations or best use of applications to render the most from the efforts of the stakeholders? In my mind, the following makes the shortlist.

Applications to;

> Inspire deeper conversations
> Allow for more controls over the filtering of information
> Verify the authenticity of sources
> Encourage the portability of information across domains
> Increase associative properties between people, places, things, tasks, situations, and information
> Enable the highlighting, bookmarking, linking, and sharing of information within documents

If you look hard enough you will find examples of these technologies in the corners of the web waiting for a framework to value the user over the provider. From the thoughtful and deep conversations surfacing from startup Cake.co's social network to a redefinition of skill development through the immersive and associative properties of Microsoft's Hololens, innovative technologies exist to empower the role of the stakeholder in the market. What could be done to invite communities of innovators both small and large into helping build the future of a decentralized web?

Regardless of whether the information is rendered through a computer screen, smartphone, tablet, smartwatch, or in the future smart glasses, windows, or mirrors, the experiences collected and shared could define who we are and who we could become. When stakeholders lack the proper tools to harness these experiences for the betterment of their own realities they will always be under-served in the market.

The current iteration of the web compromises user's identities and is a distractive force of popups and experiences failing to capture the true potential of the user weighing heavily on the promise of self-interests engaging fully in a marketplace of ideas and goods. The Solid framework and what can be built on top of it is a great start toward fixing this by moving controls and protections over to the user for a web more representative of the stakeholder but structure is not the only ingredient in a decentralized connection to elevate the role of the stakeholder.

Decentralized Artificial Intelligence
If the decentralized web is the culture in a petri dish of collective knowledge, decentralized artificial intelligence could be the catalyst or the cheese in a mousetrap of inquiry. Artificial intelligence, not as a crutch for the human condition, but as a lever requiring human effort for the stakeholder to help balance the scales of the free market. Where centralized artificial intelligence is home to massive applications only affordable to the likes of a Facebook, Google, scientific

institution, or governmental body; decentralized AI is an open and distributed framework allowing small scale deployments outside the control of large-scale corporate domains. What is possible when a group of precocious high schoolers harness advanced AI toolsets to help their community members crowdsource mental health solutions or farmers find a new organic compound to maximize crop yields through a crowdsourced initiative to tap into the minds of engaged learners.

Ben Goertzel and the team at SingularityNet.IO are leading the charge in this space by building a decentralized framework to tap into an unmined marketplace of knowledge to elevate user interests within the exchange. A democratic toolset to bring the power of artificial intelligence to the will of the user over the command of the provider. What is healthier for the market, one thousand developers creating AI solutions for one thousand use cases across one thousand domains or one thousand developers creating an AI solution for one use case within one domain?

The latter may be healthier for shareholder growth but how could it be argued this better serves the self-interests of the user. Just as the decentralized web could inspire a distribution of labor beyond a division of labor, decentralized AI could inspire a distribution of knowledge beyond a division of knowledge. A distribution of knowledge leveraging sensor data to increase situational awareness for the benefit of users, parse and analyze words to help users find what moves them the most, help users mine the digital landscape to leverage the potential of their self-interests to resonate in the market, or help validate the authenticity of sources shared or to share.

But out of all the possible applications tapping into the promise of decentralized artificial intelligence, Singularitynet's concept of Offer Networks (https://youtu.be/427hMX2LQqA) stands out to me. Where the current exchange is dominated by primarily extracting monetary value from the market, a decentralized offer network adds the value of extracting skills, knowledge, and possessions from the exchange outside the influence of a central authority.

In an offer network, AI would serve as a means to optimize self-worth between what is offered and what is needed or desired. An exchange based on the currency of self-worth paying dividends to a connected society when and only when the connection is free from centralized control.

Ben Goertzel refers to this as moving toward a post-money economy which may not please those in control of the flow of money but may revolutionize the way stakeholders participate in the market in the future. When I imagine Offer Networks, I often think of Jon Bon Jovi's Soul Kitchen restaurant in New Jersey,

cnn.com/2017/02/09/entertainment/iyw-jon-bon-jovi-jbj-soul-kit chen-trnd/index.html

where the hungry clean dishes in trade for a square meal. An analog equivalent of technology reaching inside human capabilities to serve self while meeting others needs or desires. If connected purposefully, what could a stakeholder provide to meet the specific needs of another? With a skill? An idea? A task? A different outlook? An item? An answer to a question? An exchange based less on one's station in life and more on one's interest in engaging with it reaching beyond physical or mental limitations or societal perceptions.

An alignment of an offer not limited by proximity or conventional modes of an exchange tied to linear monetary rules but fueled by a non-linear alignment of interests assisted by AI. A currency of self-worth traded in a free market of possibilities engaged around the principals of money but not defined by it.

Money will always be necessary to buy goods and services but under the current model stakeholder interests remain muted by the static forces of a monetary exchange. In theory, offer networks will liberate stakeholders from the confines of a two-dimensional exchange to surface and validate interests and capabilities from within the individual and into the exchange.

What task, skill, or information could a single welfare mother provide to an apartment complex in exchange for a reduction in her rent? How could AI align the offer with the need? Could the government provide an offset on this voucher with verification of her effort? Is this not a just use of labor in a free market? How many other scenarios could there be between people, between people and businesses, between businesses, and between people and their government representatives?

With roughly half of the world's population connected to the internet and rising, opportunities are within reach and lie within each of us to impact real human progress. No amount of money will ever move society forward like billions of stakeholders being useful in a connected world.

Blockchain
At some level, the core of the technologies described above speaks to the fundamentals of blockchain technology where

the decentralization of the connection is carried out through a distributed ledger to empower consensus amongst users with information shared. The following quotes from an article Blockchain and Decentralized Consensus

https://medium.com/orbs-network/blockchain-and-decentralized-consensus-108845a091cb

summarize the concept of Blockchain and consensus ~ "Decentralized systems are distributed systems where a group of independent but equally privileged nodes operates on local information to accomplish global goals. These systems lack a central controller that exercises governance, supervision, and control over the system, thus allowing power to be distributed over the network in a more uniform and fair manner." "Consensus is a shared view of reality that is agreed upon between different parts of a system".

The last quote serving as a powerful statement toward the heart of this essay which is to build a network (market) of users (stakeholders) through consensus outside of centralized control. Currently, users on the web agree to the provider's terms of service but more often than not, control is ceded as they log into the experiences created, consumed, and shared. A binary decision forced on the user to either go all in or not, relinquishing control of experiences in trade for new ones. But just as ant colonies communicate directly with each other as a collaborative effort outside instruction from the queen ant, as described in Steven Johnson's book Emergence

amazon.com/Emergence-Connected-Brains-Cities-Software-ebook/dp/B008TRUBLY, blockchain offers a rethinking of the pathways between human experiences. Not through a centralized consensus of the majority pushed to users but as a distribution of experiences based on individual consensus pushed from users outside the purview of the queen ant.

In theory, in a blockchain, the more users individually connect the more powerful the connection would become. Imagine one million users connected from all over the world collaborating around ideas to help the poor lift themselves out of poverty. A chain representing users from all conceivable backgrounds and interests adding ideas, sources, votes, funding, and new potential connections to local, regional, country, or global chains.

Where both monetary value and the value of effort would be aligned in the exchange based on the merits of individual contributions outside the confines of siloed experiences forming new pathways of granular transactions in service of finding and funding solutions. From crowdsourcing talent to help develop skills in local communities, pooling micro-funding to clean up blighted neighborhoods, or incentivizing self-help through the trading of utility tokens, humanitarianism could see a rise in the role of the individual stakeholder through the secure and distributive nature of blockchain technology.

In a TED talk on How the Blockchain is Changing Money and Business (https://www.youtube.com/watch?v=Pl8OIkkwRpc), Dan Tapscott spoke about an internet of information evolving to an internet of value through blockchain technology, where the ownership of experiences, objects, money, and land would become immutably attached to the owner. Mr. Tapscott used an example of how 70% of land ownership throughout the world is considered tenuous where another party could dispute ownership due to poor record-keeping.

Maybe this does not seem like much of an issue from a 1st world perspective but it does cut to the core of what is at stake when what we own is not attached to our own identity with no recourse to protect what is ours. What is possible in a future less reliant on intermediaries to maintain trust in the market and more reliant on self in the areas of philanthropy, business, science, health, government, and community development? Where a reliance on peer-to-peer insight rather than institutional oversight could be a catalyst for prosperity.

Admittedly, the Blockchain protocol has a ways to go to fulfill the promise of becoming a foundational technology for the future of the web as the tech remains energy-intensive and overly complicated. For now, cryptocurrency is the darling of the blockchain space reserved for crypto miners with deep pockets and code junkies with a penchant for puzzles but the real potential for human progress lies within the underlying fabric of blockchain technology. An environment more closely aligned with the natural human connection and the possibilities that lie within the depths of it. Which is why it should be incumbent upon thought leaders, legislators, investors, and the tech community at large to help drive these technologies forward.

Such as with Wikipedia co-founder, Larry Sanger's address

youtube.com/watch?v=rTiPxYCS6yw&feature=youtu.be

to a blockchain developer group where he asks what can be done to make the tech more accessible and usable to increase adoption. Or through congressional engagement such as with the Blockchain Promotion Act of 2019

modernconsensus.com/regulation/united-states/eyeing-the-fut ure-us-congress-moves-to-define-blockchain-and-cryptocurre ncy/

setting a requirement for the commerce department to establish a recommended definition of distributed ledger technology within one year. Or through the continued experimentation and development of technologies using elements of the blockchain protocol such as Etherium's Dapps, Everipedia's Blockchain Dictionary, Orb's Hybrid Blockchain, SingularityNet's Decentralized AI, Inrupt's Decentralized Web, and countless other innovative solutions harnessing the potential of distributive technologies.

But imagine a future where we have the world laid in front of and around us through VR, AR, and spatial computing. Where the speed of the connection removes the limits of what we experience. Where AI will predict what we know before we know it. Now imagine these technologies carried out in a non-distributive way where central authorities optimize these experiences outside the interests of the stakeholders. If we think the information flow is amplified and noisy today we are in for a rude awakening in what will be rendered in the future if the connection is not grounded to the interests of the users.

If we are looking for a cleaner, more equal, more just world, we might want to think about how we see it first as this influences how we act. Is it a trustworthy view or are we being manipulated by the fog of media elevating the whims of the masses over the inspired actions of the individual? Historically, the human connection has never had a mechanism to fold trust into the exchange the way it may be possible through a peer to peer relationship between users, objects, money, services, and information. Blockchain may turn out to be this mechanism by emerging and converging self-interests purposefully and securely into a market of ideas, goods, and services. A potential new paradigm extending value beyond the worth of possessions to the value of self-worth.

In closing

Every human being regardless of their station in life has a value of exchange residing inside. EVERYONE!! Could they solve a problem for someone else? Could they finish a task for another? Could they teach another from their mistakes or their successes? Could they entertain, resolve, or inspire? Sometimes the exchange would hold monetary value. Sometimes philanthropic. Sometimes just a simple exchange of information, possessions or capabilities. But the more the interests of the participants become aligned with each other, the more likely the exchange will validate the efforts of the giver and enrich the receiver. An exchange adding value from the pursuit of self-interest, which is the core tenet of a healthy free market.

This increase in value between both parties in the exchange is what is possible through a decentralized connection in a free market, aligning self-interests rather than influencing them through a centralized connection. Where a centralized connection favors a monetary exchange, a decentralized connection would favor an exchange of monetary, philanthropic, and human value. For those who argue against the necessity of technology to move this forward, imagine people who completely understand the intricacies of all of your value propositions, now imagine the likelihood they are all your next-door neighbors. For those who argue for the status quo, look around…is this the best the market can do for human progress?

This essay is not an affront on the road to prosperity but an exploration into bringing more stakeholders onto the road. Now that the technology is able to render a decentralized connection, what can be done to encourage the building of applications to elevate the role of the stakeholder? Decentralization alone is not the answer as there are many examples of decentralization used for ill-gotten gains but there is a symbiotic relationship between a distributed connection and the human connection that could serve humanity well if stakeholders are given the proper toolset. Tools to help uncover the best parts of what it is to be human. To place their hands of self-interest on the levers of the market to engage a community of ideas, services, and goods.

What could be discovered and exchanged in the self-interests of the poor, the ostracized, the forgotten, the disadvantaged, or even the rich or the advantaged? What could be found within self regardless of race, color, or creed? Ultimately this is a human problem but the stakeholder will never achieve parity with the shareholder when they are not demanding more from the technology representing their interests, expect more from their government representatives to write legislation to protect their data rights, and encourage investments in technologies to not only carry a monetary reward but a societal one as well.

Whether delivering search results tuned to the explicit interests of the user (outside provider influence), aligning opportunities with user capabilities through distributive AI, building intuitive interfaces to engage and protect the interests of both young and old, or building apps to optimize rather than commoditize human interests, an opportunity exists for the stakeholder to become a driving force in the market to balance out a reliance on shareholder growth. A dream outside the reach of Adam Smith and other enlightenment thinkers of his day due to the limitations of the human connection but within the grasp of those who dare to challenge the status quo today.

These are the stakeholders who will change the world for the better. Not through technology alone or the rhetorical promises of big tech but by identifying, creating, and using technologies to empower the human condition. These will be the stakeholders who dare to put their hands on the lever of the market to demand an equal stake in its success. A success based on a value of contribution coming from deep within the exchange rather than being influenced by it .

Chapter 9
Hail, Hail The Robo Taxi Is Almost Here. Are We Ready?
Originally *Published 10/23/19*

Elon Musk predicting 1,000,000 robo taxis

engadget.com/2019-04-22-tesla-elon-musk-self-driving-robo-t axi.html

on the road by 2020? Admittedly this does seem a bit far fetched but with 5.6 million electric vehicles on the road worldwide

thedriven.io/2019/02/13/there-are-now-5-6-million-electric-car s-on-the-road-up-64-from-last-year/

with the Tesla Model 3 as the world's best-selling all-electric vehicle model statista.com/topics/2086/tesla/ it is wise not to count Elon Musk out. But whether it is 2020, 2021, 2025 or 2030 it is difficult to argue a future of driverless cars is not upon us. To me, this is significant beyond a measure of convenience and safety but a societal rethinking that could change the nature of work, open new doors of discovery, and alter the future planning of our cities for the better. A new means of moving people more intently and purposefully through the real world while reducing the environmental cost of moving them. No doubt many will worry about a future without their hands on the wheel but seeds of progress are rarely easily understood at first.

"One of the most contemptible soul-destroying and devitalizing pursuits that the ill-fortune of misguided humanity has ever imposed upon its credulity."~~~C.M. Joad – British Philosopher on the arrival of the automobile.

So what are the risks to mitigate and opportunities to explore in a driverless future and how could this new reality propel a better future forward?

RISKS

Displacing drivers

There is no way around the fact that millions of professional drivers in the U.S. alone will be displaced. A reality bearing down heavily on local, regional, and national economies. Yes, it is likely the driverless industry will create new jobs as demand grows and jobs will not disappear overnight but it should be incumbent on the industry to invest in retraining and job placement programs for displaced drivers as the market evolves.

Safety Compromised?

Safety is also a significant risk attached to the driverless industry as automated vehicles begin to assimilate into the flow of traffic throughout the world. But through advancements in sensor technology, artificial intelligence, and data collected from millions of hands-free miles driven, it is only a matter of time before tech beats out the limited awareness of the human driver.

Discovery Thwarted

Removing the steering wheel is continually offered as a solution for driverless vehicles but beyond the obvious risk of being taken hostage by your car, there are much more nuanced risks involved. Yes destinations can be programmed and voice commands given but how do you articulate serendipity? Hailing a Robo taxi to a destination is one thing but as driverless vehicles become ubiquitous taking our hands off of choice could allow for our journeys to be influenced by outside forces.

So where do the opportunities lie in harnessing the potential of driverless tech to empower the commuter experience? To literally help drive the human experience forward?

OPPORTUNITIES

Raising Prospects of Low Wage Earners
A reduction in commuter cost per mile could help low-income workers find new opportunities to increase wages. As transportation costs continue to fall based on the efficiencies of the driverless model, (15 cents/mile estimated by some)

www.sciencedirect.com/science/article/pii/S0967070X173008 11

opportunities could surface to lift the disadvantaged into this connection of movement. Whether it is a low wage worker being able to take a job they could affordably commute to, supplement their income with local gigs not possible with a car payment and gas expenditures, or allow someone on a fixed income to make a medical appointment on the other side of town, the reduced barriers of cost alone could help emerge capabilities from commuters like no other time in the history of transportation.

Cities Reimagined
How will cities evolve - How Self-Driving Cars Might Transform City Parking - IEEE Spectrum

spectrum.ieee.org/autonomous-parking

when parking is no longer attached to the destination? A new reality bringing both risks and opportunities where driverless cars in constant circulation could increase traffic congestion but at the same time free up valuable real estate for pedestrian-friendly common areas and sidewalks. Either way, commuters will be spending less time parking vehicles and walking to destinations and more time engaging around their destinations which could inspire community-focused planning. Could we see a resurgence of Main Street style planning with cobblestone streets heavily populated by mom and pop retailers and niche service providers? Only time will tell.

Workforce Redefined
As the workforce begins to adopt driverless tech, work will become less of a place and more of a journey, especially as the gig and sharing economy continues to break apart conventional means of work as a container for workers to fit into. I would call this more of a catalyst for progress than a disrupter of industry as when labor becomes more productive and engaged in the marketplace how could industry not benefit? Whether workers are spending more quality facetime with customers, vendors, or associates, are liberated from the confines of cubicles and bullpens, or supplementing their income by leasing out their vehicle

usatoday.com/story/tech/2019/04/23/elon-musk-says-tesla-ow ners-could-make-30-000-robotaxi-network/3549652002/

to a driverless fleet, how could it be argued better work will not come from better engagement and better work environments for workers? Driverless tech has the potential to reimagine a future of workers empowered through mobility, so the question is will employers embrace this as a means to improve the quality of the worker and customer experiences, or fight it to protect measures of control?

Environmental Impact Reduced
For every autonomous vehicle to hit the streets running off of electric power or fuel cells optimized for efficiency of operation through route choice and acceleration patterns, a reduction in environmental impact should occur. Even though energy consumption may increase

theworld.org/stories/2017-04-18/driverless-cars-could-either-be-scary-or-great-environment

as more miles are traveled through the convenience and affordability of self-driving automation, pollutants from emissions will decrease as gasoline engines are replaced with clean-burning alternatives. The birth of a new form of decentralized energy distribution may also arise as autonomous vehicles begin to transfer excess energy collected and generated between destinations. In the end, an increase in demand for energy-efficient, clean-burning driverless vehicles could usher in a new era of transportation serving as more of a partner with mother earth than a competitor.

Discovery Empowered
I write about the emergent capabilities of technology to empower human engagement and see driverless technologies as a means to encourage discovery in the real world. How many historical markers are within driving distance? How many live venues? How many interesting lectures? How many friends or family members are within driving distance but are not visited due to limitations of cost, time, or motivation? A reduction in cost per commuter mile,

replacing drive time with productive time, and improving the commuter experience online could remove these limitations but influence wielded outside of commuter interests could weigh heavily on this potential.

Interests possibly co-opted as the attention of the driver moves away from the road to car windows and smart devices overlaying information over their journey. Will this overlay become a pop-up laden, ad-heavy experience as we see with the centralized web today or a resonant experience where the commuter is empowered by the connection rather than being controlled by it?

In Closing
People will continue to drive well into the future just as people will continue to read paper bound books but as driverless tech continues to evolve into our communities, driving will move from more of a need to a choice. This, I believe will help usher in a new era of a cleaner and more resonant model of transportation engaging and empowering commuters rather than distracting them. A future optimized for the safety and inspired actions of commuters while reducing the environmental impact of their travels.

What is possible when commutes become opportunities to learn, to be entertained, and to be more purposeful rather than a means to an end? What is possible when people are spending more time walking and exploring around their destinations than looking for parking? What is possible when the power of the online connection motivates commuters to discover the real world more intently? Admittedly, there are many obstacles in the way of a better commuter experience through driverless technologies but as with any revolutionary societal breakthroughs, the journey can be a bit messy. The question is what we can learn from past mistakes to make certain we are ready for this future?

Chapter 10
Ebook Embargo On Libraries Is Only The Tip Of The Iceberg
Originally Published 11/14/19

As of November 1st, 2019 MacMillan Publishing, one of the largest print publishers in the world, placed an 8-week embargo on libraries purchasing more than one copy of new release eBooks limiting an entire branch to loan out one eBook at a time to library patrons. This coupled with the publishing community beginning to limit perpetual access to eBooks and audiobooks, in general, should serve as a warning for what is about to come with the continued siloing and commoditization of information. A new reality favoring publishers and aggregators over creators and consumers closing in not only on the expressions of authors but the reportage of journalists, songs of artists, and the visions of filmmakers.

As much as I like my Netflix subscription and my son likes his Spotify subscription, I have to wonder what the future will bring when important news stories and creative expressions are fenced-in through subscription models and exclusive content deals priced out of reach of the average wage earner. Is there any doubt the total cost of information consumption will rise as more information providers climb on board the gravy train of the subscription model? Consumer choice limited to which silo to choose rather than which creator of information to choose. The flow of information limited at the expense of the consumer. Sound familiar?

So when a top-five international book publisher picks a fight

https://slate.com/business/2019/09/e-book-library-publisher-buying-controversy-petition.html with 138,000 librarians over an 8-week release window, one has to wonder if this is the canary in the coal mine warning of what is to come. In an open letter

d1x9nywezhk0w2.cloudfront.net/wp-content/uploads/2019/10/29160131/A-Letter-from-John-Sargent-.pdf

to librarians, MacMillan publishing CEO John Sargent offered, "We believe the very rapid increase in the reading of borrowed ebooks decreases the perceived economic value of a book," and "To borrow a book in those days required transportation, returning the book, and paying those pesky fines when you forgot to get them back on time. In today's digital world there is no such friction in the market."

Apparently perception and friction are the drivers aligning authors' hard work with the interests of consumers in this new era of connectivity? Not to discount the necessity of profitability but when profit begins to step on discovery how will the consumer and the publishing industry not suffer? Yes, there is a scalability issue for publishers in consumers checking out a free eBook through a library portal online rather than physically picking up a book from a local library but is this the fight to pick to prove a point? A fight with a community of highly engaged readers who have shown in studies to purchase books after reading at the library.

"50% of all library users report purchasing books by an author they were introduced to in the library." Patron Profiles, 2011

panoramaproject.org/news/2019/7/26/macmillan-announces-library-ebook-embargo-new-lending-terms

I don't believe this is a fight that will be won by either side. Maybe a better use of resources and time would be for publishers to spend more time experimenting with rental models, previewing sections based on reader interests, and better ad models to capture the interest of the reader against native content. It would be hard to argue growth in eBook sales over the years has met industry expectations but is the stagnation more about pirated content or a lack of innovation? This push by publishers to squeeze libraries over eBook sales leads me to believe the issue is with the latter which is also a reflection on the current information ecosystem as a whole.

A system incorporating conventional tactics of provider controls over a rapidly evolving connection allowing the user to expect more. This dissonance between publishers/aggregators and creators/consumers is what we are facing today limiting the reach of information to positively impact the whole of society. Will the Macmillan publishing companies of the world continue to talk or begin to listen to help right this ship? The Titanic missed the enormity of a situation as most of the threat was hidden from plain sight from a distracted crew. Are information publishers/aggregators about to make the same mistake?

Additional reading on this subject:

ebooksforall.org/index.php/get-involved

www.publishersweekly.com/pw/by-topic/industry-news/librarie s/article/81596-macmillan-ceo-john-sargent-we-re-not-trying-t o-hurt-libraries.html

d1x9nywezhk0w2.cloudfront.net/wp-content/uploads/2019/10/ 29160131/A-Letter-from-John-Sargent-.pdf

panoramaproject.org/news/2019/7/26/macmillan-announces-li
brary-ebook-embargo-new-lending-terms

kcls.org/blogs/post/publishers-decision-to-limit-ebook-access-i
s-bad-news-for-library-patrons

Chapter 11
Advertising's Lost Opportunities
Originally Published 12/15/19

I guess I am on this kick again. Just can't shake it. I wrote an essay back in March (Chapter 4: Emerging Consumer Interests through Tunable Ads) on this and the continued barrage of non relevant ads into my digital footprint is keeping the argument alive for me. I believe I must have seen this ad from HostGator 50 times on different media platforms in the last week. I have to ask – what in the hell does this have to do with me.

Not the service. I actually might be in the market for a service like this in the future. No~ the advertisement. Granted, this ad may speak to the interests of many out there which is fantastic. No judgment whatsoever. It just doesn't speak to me. It actually turns me off the service. Are there any ads that do the same thing for you? They are lost opportunities for engagement in my mind. I could see the necessity of shotgun ads in the past before technology could tune images and moving images to my interests but here we are knocking on the doorstep of 2020 (The future by all accounts) and I am met with this?

How do you solve this? You allow me to keep my interests stored in a personal and private silo where advertisers have to knock on my door and ask my explicit permission to advertise to me. I would say yes as long as they met the criteria for providing advertisement of services that match the interests I designated. And if there were an AI assistant in my silo, I might even be open to discovering interests I never thought of before and therefore related products and services. I argue under this model, businesses who care enough to understand their customers could increase sales.

So now HostGator would be competing for my interests rather than my clicks. Could they create a library of ads built around an ecosystem of interests that could be aligned with my personal silo? In the near future, yes. But not until personal silos are a thing. More of a chicken and egg argument. This is the reason why in my opinion it is important to create technologies where my interests and activities hide behind a personal silo. Build this and they will come (hopefully). Tim Berners Lee and Inrupt are working on personal silos through their Solid POD framework and I know others are working on similar tech.

Unless we would like to keep the doors of our cars, our homes, and our bank accounts open permanently, I just don't know why we would want to keep the doors of our experiences open. It will never be perfect but once we begin to regain control of these experiences, I believe the opportunities for engagement and commercial transactions are limitless. They would just serve the interests of the consumer more than the provider. But isn't that still a win for all involved? Is it advertising if we are interested? Wouldn't this change in perception be healthy for purveyors of goods and services?

One way to find out. Let's build it. What do **WE** have to lose?

Chapter 12
Emergent Innovation - The Next Frontier
Originally Published 1/13/20

"Emergent Innovation is synonymous with breakthroughs, disruption, radical ideas, paradigm-shifting results, raw novelty, and market creation." ~~ FreshConsulting.com

A list of 20 current Emergent Innovators can be found below this essay

Look around. They could be in your community. At your workplace sitting next to you. Across the field at the baseball stadium. At your church. In the ghetto. At your child's play. Across your dinner table. Who or what is it? A person, group or organization with an innovative approach to thinking or a game-changer of an idea to help improve the human condition to emerge from a marketplace of ideas to make a difference if given the chance.

Innovations to;

> Create better opportunities for self-actualization
> Promote a cleaner environment
> Improve physical and mental health
> Improve understanding between people and communities
> Increase the value of the exchange in the free market by bringing more people into the benefits of it.

Of course, emergent innovations are not only the domain of improving the human condition as products can be improved upon and productivity increased to help the bottom line. But to me and hopefully many others, the concept of emergence

speaks better to a role of innovation serving something
greater than only a bottom line.

In Steven Johnson's book Emergence, he writes about the
power of ant colonies working together for the benefit of the
colony outside the control of the queen ant. Each ant
innovating and communicating directly with other ants to grow
and protect their colony. Common interests emerging from the
efforts of the individual ant in service of themselves and their
community. Just as with ant colonies, what is possible when
the capabilities of humans working solo or with others
innovate in service of themselves and their communities
regardless of market forces or outside influences? Where
innovation emerges from human inspiration and will.

How do we get there? The path to progress in my estimation
is to move the lens of innovation from the macro to the micro
and from the expectations of short term gains to long term
impact where opportunities to affect real change might be
found. But this will only happen when we start to proactively
look for Emergent Innovators in our midst to encourage, fund,
and remove roadblocks in their way.

Does a mindset to build this reality currently exist? Certainly.
Just look at the growth of the social impact investment
community

causeartist.com/changing-the-world-through-social-impact-inv
esting/

where investments are made on both monetary value and
social impact to fund opportunities in the market traditionally
passed on. Look at the arrival of Certified B Corporations

bcorporation.net/en-us/find-a-b-corp/

and Benefit Corporations to balance purpose and profit within a marketplace to positively impact workers, customers, suppliers, community, and the environment. And look at the efforts made by organizations such as the Bill and Melinda Gates Foundation to tackle some of the world's biggest challenges without chasing ROI.

What is possible when you apply this momentum toward the discovery of untapped talent and ideas to help turn the tide toward a future more representative of human potential than the course we are currently on? I believe great things are possible but where are the opportunities to be found to help move this forward?

Government
Could governments become more involved to help identify and fund Emergent Innovators living among us? Just as governments helped push humans into space and build the backbone of the internet, what could be done to help cut red tape and authorize the funding of programs to incentivize those who dare to break the mold of the status quo.

Private Capital
Could social impact investing become woven into the fabric of philanthropic efforts to work more on root causes limiting progress rather than the symptoms?

Organizations
Could consulting firms, NGOs, and organizations increase their focus on identifying innovative thinkers within their ranks to experiment on bold new ideas rather than sure money bets?

Technology

Could technologists grow their dual role as both a toolset for emergent innovators to build solutions as well as build tech to help innovators become discovered?

Indeed quite a few "What ifs" but as with any frontier to explore, progress will not come without changes in behaviors. Although, if there were ever a new frontier to explore to pay large dividends for human progress it would be to tap the potential of the human spirit waiting in all corners of the world to rise to the challenge. They will most certainly fall and fail repeatedly but adding legions of innovators from all walks of life will only increase the odds of success.

But will they be easily found? Probably not as how often does genius arrive in a nicely wrapped package. What would be the chances of walking past Nikola Tesla digging ditches in 1884 after he was fired from the Edison Company? Or leaving unimpressed after talking to a Swiss patent clerk with the crazy hair when filing for a patent in 1905. Ask yourself, could somebody in your midst today have the next great idea to move humanity forward? Are they a teacher, a student, a coder, a janitor, a CEO bogged down with meetings and margin calls, or an upstart organization with a radical idea for progress?

What is possible when the spirit of innovation reaches beyond convention, stereotypes, and profit motives to harness the capabilities of members within society to contribute toward a society more reflective of a wider swath of capabilities? When innovation reaches past income level, gender, ethnicity, creed, education, or age to begin to dig deeper into the toolbox of human potential. Who knows, the next frontier for human progress could be right before our eyes.

Below is a list of innovators whether they are people or organizations I believe speak well to the ideas behind emergent innovation.

Emergent Innovators

Morgan Vague
independent.co.uk/climate-change/news/plastic-eating-bacteria-pollution-crisis-environment-microbes-student-a8423146.html
A student may have found a solution to one of the world's most urgent environmental crises – breeding bacteria capable of "eating" plastic and potentially breaking it down into harmless by-products.

Bill & Melinda Gates Foundation
gatesfoundation.org/
From attempting to eradicate polio globally to reimagining nuclear energy there's no better test case of emergent innovation than through the efforts of the Bill & Melinda Gates Foundation

Inrupt.com
Tim Berners Lee, the Solid Project, and the team at Inrupt are reimagining the world wide web as a decentralized connection to put the user back in control of the world wide web.

Dandelion Energy
dandelionenergy.com/
Replace a home's existing air conditioning and heating equipment with a powerful heat pump and safe, underground pipes to move heat between the earth and the home.

Adrian Lopez Velarde and Marte Cazarez
vegnews.com/2019/11/two-guys-in-mexico-just-created-vegan
-leather-from-cactus
Mexican entrepreneurs Adrian Lopez Velarde and Marte
Cazarez, created a clean alternative for leather from animal
hides to reduce a reliance on the killing of animals.

Sana Health
sana.io/
The first non-invasive bio-therapeutic device providing lasting
relief for chronic pain sufferers.

NovaMeat
novameat.com/
The world's first 3D-printed plant-based beefsteak in 2018

FIAIM
flaimsystems.com/#Research%20Development
Uses an immersive virtual reality environment – combined
with a patented haptics feedback system, breathing
apparatus, and heated personal protective clothing – to
provide a unique training experience for firefighters.

Sea Around Us
SeaAroundUs.org
Tracks fisheries, ecosystems, and biodiversity using open
data to examine private and industrial fishing around the
world.

Vanguard Renewables
vanguardrenewables.com/
Provides farm powered organics to energy lifecycle to solve
organic waste disposal challenges, generate renewable

natural gas or renewables electricity, and support the American farmer.

Trust Circle
trustcircle.co
Utilizes AI-driven Social Emotional Learning programs to improve wellbeing for all.

Turner Impact Capital
turnerimpact.com
One of the nation's largest and fastest-growing social impact investment firms positioned to invest up to $3 billion in real estate solutions to address daunting societal challenges across the U.S.

Grameen Bank
microfinancefocus.com/5-microfinance-pioneers-who-change d-bop-finance-landscape
Advanced to the forefront of a burgeoning world movement toward eradicating poverty through micro-lending.

Thorn.org
thorn.org/
Building technology to defend children from sexual abuse.

Life Dreamer
imnovation-hub.com/water/a-new-approach-in-desalination-lif e-dreamer-project
A new approach in desalination could make use of up to 90% of treated seawater

Code for America
codeforamerica.org
Puts the two biggest levers (technology & government) to

improve people's lives at scale and help make government work in the digital age.

Indus
dezeen.com/2019/09/21/bio-id-lab-indus-algae-tiles-water
Created an algae wall to purify polluted water without harmful chemicals

Chapter 13
Introduction To The Emergence
Originally Published 9/24/23

Welcome to the inaugural episode of The Emergence asking the question – what is possible when we are connected and in control?

My name is J.Paul Duplantis and I am a podcaster and essayist on the intersection between technology and human interests. I am on a mission to create awareness, help identify, and help build technologies to tap into human potential by removing barriers within the flow of information. I am not on the left. I am not on the right. I am curious and I believe communication technology can do a better job of uniting more than dividing to create a better environment for progress for all without sacrificing the innovative spirit of the free market.

This podcast will be an evolution. This first episode will be an essay to set up ideas I would like to explore throughout this podcast series and will be a combination of conversations with interesting people around these ideas, readings of my essays, and me walking around riffing freestyle on ideas I believe speak well to the concept of The Emergence.

But before I get into the idea of the Emergence let me share who I am to give you an idea where this madness is coming from. I'm a 56-year-old guy with a background in marketing, management, technology, sales, consulting, and recruiting. Before the early 90s, my passions lied more in filmmaking and music but the internet happened and my soul was moved toward the idea of what would be possible when people were connected purposefully. Thankfully the creative side has never left me as I would consider myself more of a creative thinker than a technical thinker.

But I have to admit this shift in interests served as more of a distraction from building a career than anything else as the more possibilities I could see from a truly connected marketplace, the more frustrated I became especially when Web 2.0 started to build walls around the open connection. I even tried to build out these ideas through a company I helped launch called Quired which ended up as a side hustle only deepening my frustration.

Certainly, if I could see it I should have been able to build it. Well, that couldn't have turned out to be further from the truth. The problem was I didn't know what I was looking for. I had a vision but it was blurred and I didn't have a plan. The most frustrating part was I knew something was there. I mean the technology was arriving but the top-heavy controls were weighing heavily on the potential that could come from it so I effectively gave up on the dream.

It was 7 years ago, almost to the day of me recording this episode, that I gave up on this dream and decided to hunker down and focus on a 9 to 5 job. Fortunately for me, I landed in a place where I love the owners and the people I work with and have been able to work in areas of marketing, information systems, processes, and just being there to help which is one of my favorite activities, so no complaints.

But about 4 years ago, I got the itch again as I saw the amazing developments happening within the communication technology space so I thought I would at least be more consistent about writing on these ideas. I mean what was happening with VR, AR, mobile computing, the internet of things and AI were blowing me away, so I started to dig in. I even consulted for a VR company in Scottsdale for a while on the side and witnessed a small startup struggling with a revolutionary, yet very new technology. And it wasn't until I walked into a bookstore about 3 years ago that I finally was able to make sense of what was in my head for the last 20 or so years.

True story. I started to meditate around this time to help cope with my frustration that had been building to a crescendo and one day before walking into a Bookman's bookstore in Phoenix, I meditated to help understand what this madness was. What was this idea I had been chasing? What was the methodology behind the idea? Yes, people were connected like no other time before and they were controlled by it but what was the solution or at least the path forward? I felt maybe at least I could find something I could personalize to help me put these ideas into a better context for others to relate to.

As I walked into the bookstore, I just told myself the first book I touched was going to be some form of an answer. I seriously had no idea why I was doing something so foolish but hey we are all human and I needed a true north badly. So I roamed and found a section I felt might speak to me, walked forward, and without looking put my hand on the book **Emergence: The Connected Lives of Ants, Brains, Cities, and Software by Steven Johnson**

Scouts honor and this is the absolute truth. So an aha moment at 52. I guess Ray Kroc stumbled across the McDonald's franchise around the same age after swimming in obscurity so I figured if I wasn't going to be a small part of revolutionizing the connection at least I knew what the idea was. So what was so special about this book? I was immediately struck by one of the stories in the book about ant colonies using pheromones or chemical traces as signals between each other. Signals that would help ants determine the best places to bury their dead, hide their food, and overall protect the colony from invaders.

Ants sending signals between each other to make decisions collectively for the betterment of themselves and the whole outside the control of the Queen ant or centralized control if you will. Where the capabilities of the ants emerged from the colony but were not directed by it. Ants working with each other, understanding each other, as well as becoming aware of common threats and opportunities.

As I read this book, my line of thinking immediately centered around the idea of what communication technology could become for humans. How could our capabilities emerge from each of us to serve ourselves and each other without a reliance on centralized forces to mitigate threats and explore opportunities? What would be the potential of our signal if we were connected emergently?

Not only to each other but with media outlets, purveyors of goods and services, and even governmental bodies. What if the connection was optimized to reach into our untapped skills, hidden talents, and explicit interests rather than only the needs of the market? A market defined by the connected not just the connection.

Obviously, there is a connection extending the reach of the human voice that exists today but this connection is highly centralized and optimized more for the exchange of monetary value than the exchange of value of the capabilities residing within the connection. I thought to myself, what would be possible when the connection was optimized for human value where individual capabilities were harnessed to inspire what I call CAPE or creativity, awareness, productivity, and empathy to feedback into the connection.

After reading this book and recognizing the technology at our disposal, I began to realize I was witnessing the potential birth of a new paradigm shift in human communication and began to see the connection differently than before. It was this idea of distance and capabilities that started to grab me. Think about it. What are the chances the most interesting person in the world to you is your next-door neighbor? What are the chances the skills and interests you possess are being fully utilized at your workplace? To me, this erasure of distance and limit on capabilities was a catalyst for rethinking the human connection.

What would be possible when barriers were removed between what people were capable of and what was expected of them dictated by the market? We all possess skills that both nature and nurture have blessed us with and mostly our locality dictates whether these skills will be utilized or not. Remove these barriers to scale globally and an exchange of value between people, businesses, and governments could be untapped to add more purpose into the exchange. An exchange of human value within a purposeful market over an exchange of monetary value in a free market.

Many might say technology already erases distance and frees capabilities when we work remotely and discover information through the web but currently, purpose seems to be more assigned to us than defined by us. I'm not attacking work, I'm attacking the institution of work when it only trades in the quantity of labor for profit. I can hear the arguments now. Yep, money needs to be made to build infrastructure and keep people employed. Got it. But has that been enough? It appears the free market is maximizing the opportunities found within the labor force to extract more value from labor than the value labor is getting from work. I admit, maybe my emergent lens is distorting my reality as to how would I know what happens inside the exchange of labor en masse but I just ask to look around. Are we emergent in the potential of our labor? Shouldn't we be?

Should the homeless person you pass on the way to work be actively engaged with the potential of their labor? We can have an easy conversation on why they are not but the more difficult conversation is could they be? Is it that "work" is not available because they don't want to work or is it the right opportunity that has not found them to fully engage their potential at some point in their life to serve as an anchor for better things to come?

I work in an area heavily populated by the homeless and ask myself daily what talents and skills are trapped inside of their situations? What would be their true capacity if opportunity not only found them but understood who they are? Not through a centralized institutional approach as we find in many workplaces and mental health care facilities but emergently to understand the human first then optimize their potential within the greater marketplace.

Think about it for a moment. In the quest to optimize the potential of labor, wouldn't mental health be at the epicenter of what is holding it back? Currently, mental health appears to be treated as more of a problem to have than a solution to find. An affliction affecting the young and the old, the poor and the rich, all genders, all races passed down genetically or behaviorally through generation after generation. When our mind is not healthy, how are we supposed to tap into our capabilities to influence the market rather than being influenced by it? Mental health is the moonshot for The Emergence as I believe there are technologies and methodologies on the horizon to not only repair physical damage to the brain but to help people better relate their mental state with the world around them. Solutions not coming from a centralized marketplace leveraged for the benefit of the provider but an emergent market to help improve the signal within and among those responsible for the very existence of the market they are a part of.

In the grand scheme of things, The Emergence is not only about communication technology, it is about rethinking the toolset we are using to tap into human potential. Do we think the current top-down centralized approach in the way we work, the way we handle our mental health, and the way we consume and share information is ultimately healthy for all of society? Is the well-being of all of society important? Or is it only for the strong and the resilient?

To me, The Emergence gets to the core of the question of what is possible when we are connected and in control? Where each of us is more influential in building our better realities regardless of the color of our skin, our gender, or our level of income. Where we are less dependent on institutions dictating who we should become and become more in tune with who we are and what we all have to offer. Is it better for society to rely more on social programs than on social tools? I believe there should be a healthy mix – as a reliance on programs to treat the symptom more than the cause fails to get to the root of the problems that turn into other problems and fodder for political maneuvering.

As we move past the halfway mark of connecting 7.5 billion people on planet earth, how many opportunities exist to exchange value in what people offer if the connection was free from influences outside of their interests? Seems pie in the sky but reality is soon to render a world where automation will replace a significant portion of the skills humans traditionally offer.

What then? Where will the drivers, the manufacturers, and the clerks go? A double whammy as lower-skilled jobs will be replaced with automation while the remaining higher-skilled jobs will come with a high price tag for skill development. With the cost of obtaining a university education in the U.S. surging 1,120 percent between 1978 and 2014 according to a Bloomberg report based on the Bureau of Labor Statistics data, what will the next 36 years bring to the prospect of labor? [1]. 1 Especially knowing median wages have increased 290% between 1977 and 2019, how will this reality not continue to increase the wealth gap? Is this important? It is for The Emergence.

In the dream world of The Emergence, the traditional walls of work and information silos would fall to free up the true potential of labor. Of course, I'm not talking about removing the notion of the traditional workplace but using tools to help people find new opportunities outside conventional means. Opportunities where people have a stake in the fulfillment of a need, are validated through the provision of their efforts and are compensated beyond only the profit motive of fulfilling the need. A toolset to align not only the potential of one's labor with a need but with information and experiences to help realize interests, talents, and skillsets a provider-centric marketplace based only on profit would not be motivated to find. A toolset to not only align opportunities with self-interest and situations but to help mitigate threats by empowering users with awareness and understanding of themselves and their surroundings.

This is the quest of the Emergence. To identify and create awareness of this toolset to inspire a purposeful and emergent market on top of a free market. A market to balance the interests of people with businesses and governments for all people to become more influential in building their own better realities. And if you don't agree with what I am saying and want to call me out on specifics, I absolutely want to have a dialogue to learn and grow around these ideas. But if you don't agree with the fact the system is broken or the problem is only a human one to fix then the emergence is not going to be your cup of tea I can assure you.

The Tools

So if you are still hanging in there, what is this toolset to tap into human potential for The Emergence to happen? What is the solution? I believe it is broken down into four areas.

Number 1. Laws to enforce data rights.

Number 2. Decentralized frameworks to secure and empower user data.

Number 3. Decentralized Artificial Intelligence to provide context and awareness, and

Number 4. a Decentralized application layer to allow users to tap into their own potential and that of the communities they are involved with.

So let's dig in.....

Number 1: User Data Rights

It seems clear to me that we need better laws to enforce user data as a human right to put the user in the driver seat of their own experiences. Without user data rights, applications will continue to find a way to manipulate or sell out the interests and behaviors of the users, muting the potential of the exchange by only monetizing it. The GDPR in Europe is a beginning salvo on this front but without a doubt, we need a robust set of laws to protect the information we create, consume, and share. I found an interesting article on New Legislation in the U.S. Proposing a Federal Data Protection Agency which I will link to in the podcast notes. [2]

And not only data rights for the individual but a better framework to provide free public access to government-funded data and information created by universities and institutions. Think of the sheer volume of information locked behind scholarly publications for sale and paywalls that if unlocked could drive innovative ideas for progress. Information freely available to not only academics and professionals, creating feedback loops, but for the public at large to engage with to give birth to our next great innovators to build toward a cleaner environment, more effective and affordable health care, and to help find solutions to help lift more people out of poverty. I've yet to scratch the surface on the subject of data rights and look forward to finding interesting people to have a conversation with on what is possible to move these ideas into reality.

Number 2: The Frameworks

We need to create technology to provide user controls over their information. To effectively separate user data from applications to limit the amount of control of the provider and the network over the user. There are a number of frameworks currently in development, I believe may one day render this a reality. So why is a universal decentralized framework important to secure user data rights? Because if we leave it up to each company to do the right thing, we will be let down. We always have been. This is such an incredibly wide topic I hope to have plenty of conversations in the future to help illuminate the pros and cons of decentralized frameworks.

So what is at the core behind the idea of a decentralized framework? Imagine not logging into Facebook, Apple, Google, or any other information service but granting them permission to access the experiences you create, consume or share. As opposed to you agreeing to their terms of service, they would agree with yours. I happen to have fairly extreme views on this as I believe no matter where our data resides whether it is on a web server, an email application, a game, or in a sensor if we create the experience, the experience is ours by default. Imagine playing a game of chess on a smartphone app where you are playing with 5 opponents you had met in the game.

Currently, the moves you make and the conversations you have regarding these moves are the property of the game. Should they be? Of course, the specific articulation of the game is the property of the game provider but how about the experiences contained within? What if you found a different game more suited to your tastes? Should you be able to relocate these moves and conversations to another game? Did the creator of this game pay for the experiences or the infrastructure? I argue they only paid for the representation of these experiences, not the experiences themselves. We pay for our experiences in living them, so why shouldn't we be in control of them?

Should you be able to easily move a calendar item from Google Calendar to a Facebook event or vice versa. Should you be able to easily move a tweet thread with other users into an email or text? Should you be able to easily mash up sensor data with a photo found on the web with a paragraph from a scientific study all the while retaining authorship and formatting from all the source material. I believe you should and I believe tools to be built in the future should have portability, authorship, and verifiability at its very core.

The web as we know it today is the wild west of an information exchange, allowing businesses to coop user interests with very little concern over the validity and repercussions of what is shared. Managing permissions are at the center of this better future but how this is achieved is what is proving to be incredibly difficult. How do you create a better and more secure web for people without making it more difficult for them to use and without it equally being as prone to centralized control?

Tim Berners Lee's Solid PODS framework is an interesting solution to this problem as he is the founder of the world wide web with a sincere frustration with the direction it has taken. And Solid PODS are an especially good test case for a framework to contain our data rights as it originated through a public institution (MIT) and is being deployed through a private company called Inrupt. Just as Google is a private company, when we agree to their terms of service they own our data, so why would Inrupt be any different?

So far, in theory, Solid PODS are more of a specification and methodology for other companies to use in offering their own data stores, where the PODS provider would never have access to the user's data, only serving the user as an intermediary for their data. A key feature of the Solid PODS framework would be the ability of the user to move their data between PODS providers and applications if they were ever unhappy with the service, so in theory, no one else other than the user would ever be in control of their data.

I emphasize the words in theory, because the framework has not launched as of yet, so the free market has not had a chance to sink its teeth in yet. Inrupt appears to be a private company currently but what would happen if it turned into a public company, where the interest of the shareholders would factor into the growth of the framework? Would they go as far as taking away the control of user data from the likes of Google, Facebook, Twitter, Amazon, and Apple? Do they have a strong enough of a unified front to pull this off?

I've been following the Solid PODS Dev team's progress on GitHub for over a year now and have come to realize how incredibly difficult this proposition truly is. Don't get me wrong they have some of the greatest minds and developers in the world on this but the sheer size and force of the status quo driven by big tech are staggering.

Should something of this scale be handled by a private company or a public institution? A very difficult question indeed. I don't have the answers but I do know the very notion of this idea of separating data from the application is incredibly important to how we move forward as a society. Do we want to be in control of our experiences or not? Some might be fine with just letting the market run its course, but I see this is more of a threat to the fundamentals of democracy so I guess I have a different lens on it.

Let me offer an example of what I'm talking about. So I was going back and forth with the originator of the hashtag Chris Messina on Twitter about Twitter tweeting they would provide access to an edit button on Twitter if everyone would just wear a mask during the Covid 19 crisis to save lives. [3] I posed to Chris my thoughts that this was an exercise in centralized control over a user base which was worrisome to me. He felt temporary measures of centralized control were in order.

Although I very much respect Chris' opinion, the more I thought about this, I became quite angry at the notion of a company hijacking my experiences and threatening levels of access to these experiences in trade for my social compliance. Mind you, I have no problem with people needing to wear masks for Covid 19 but if this then what next.

What will Google, Facebook, Twitter, or any other online platform decide for me in how I render my experiences in the future? What feature set will they not allow, what will they hide from me, what will they amplify for me and trade for a profit from persuasion.

Yes, I have a right to use another platform but the experiences I created, consumed, and shared within their platform don't share the same rights. The fact that Twitter could even debate the idea of allowing me to edit my information in trade for my social compliance illuminates a fundamental question for the future of human communication. Should people be in control of their experiences or should businesses and/or the government? Did the yellow pages back from yesteryear own the relationships formed and sharing of experiences with the people found in their phone book? Did US West not spend billions of dollars to build the infrastructure for people to communicate through their network and publish listings of their customers? Was a login to US West required to call one of their customers?

Yes, an agreement had to be made on terms of service for use of their system but was an agreement made to forfeit all experiences conducted on their network as well as to related advertisers? I seriously think we're going to look back in one hundred years at the communication tools we have built today and wonder how the hell did people let this happen. These are their platforms but our experiences, right?

It is my greatest wish that somehow, someway we figure out how to separate the two in the future as our musings on Twitter are the least of our problems when you think about our sensor data, medical data, web history, chat history, personal correspondence, government data, location data and on and on and on. We give them an inch they're going to take a mile. It's just what the market does.

Could the Solid framework change this reality, by moving experiences under the control of the user's domain? I certainly hope so. There is no denying, I am rooting for the Solid team and would love to have members of the team on the podcast in the future to discuss the challenges they face and what they hope to accomplish.

Another core decentralized framework to help put data into the hands of the user outside the control of centralized forces is the Blockchain framework. Even though Blockchain technology is currently known more for the cryptocurrency and the Bitcoin craze, the underlying mechanism of managing data through distributed ledgers validated through tokens could prove to revolutionize the way information is accessed, edited, and shared. A methodology to remove centralized governance from the flow of information to empower the user with authority over their data.

Currently, Blockchain technologies are power-intensive and limited in transaction speeds which is not a good recipe for a framework to revolutionize the connection, but innovations are on the horizon to help remove these barriers to help move blockchain into more of a decentralized future. One of the more interesting players on the scene is Etherium led by co-founder Vitalek Buterin. Where Bitcoin is the leader in cryptocurrency using the blockchain protocol, Etherium is the leader in creating an ecosystem beyond the management of money online to a framework to manage applications attached to a decentralized blockchain.

Ethereum 2.0 is the next iteration of the Ethereum framework to reduce the limitations of current blockchain technologies. At the heart of this is a movement away from the traditional Proof of Work model where massive computers solve puzzles to build new blocks in the chain to a model based on Proof of Stake where validators in the chain purchase Ethereum currency to add blocks to the chain. There appears to be a number of objectives with this major overhaul expected to be rolled out over a number of years to include making the chain less dependent on massive amounts of energy consumed to maintain viability and increasing transaction speeds beyond the very limiting 15 transactions per second available today.

There are several blockchain frameworks under development to include the Stellar, Hyperledger, Multichain, as well as the Elastos framework which has been making waves lately in increasing the value of their coin offerings in the space. I have to admit I get a major case of Deja Vous when I see these companies talking about the mission of their technology for the greater good all the while they focus on building monetary value through their coins.

Of course, money needs to be made to build infrastructure but is the money spent ultimately in service of the product or the end-user. Time will tell which ones will stay the course to truly decentralize and emerge users to a more resonant connection. Either way I do believe Blockchain technology is here to stay and could be a major catalyst for progress.

Without a doubt, the Solid Framework and Blockchain are not the only solutions on the horizon to give power to the user over their information. One of the missions of this podcast will be to dig deep to uncover more of these technologies and hopefully talk to founders and developers to learn how their tech will empower the user and their communities. One technology that seems interesting to me is GunDB which is a decentralized database to increase data security, reduce costs, and provide a scalable toolset for application developers to build off of.

I have been following GunDB founder Mark Nadal on Twitter for a while now and have exchanged a few tweets around his vision for the future of the web and have concluded Mark is one to keep an eye on as he is looking to harness these technologies to tackle society's biggest problems.

Number Three: The AI Layer

If there is anything as scary as it is thrilling it would be the growing reality of a connection heavily influenced by artificial intelligence. People can wish this away all they want but AI has arrived, even though we are still in relatively early days. I truly feel once quantum computing makes the jump to practical applications, we will begin to see mind-blowing applications of artificial intelligence but the question is in the future will AI be for us or against us?

Do we want to live in a black mirror episode or do we want to harness the amazing capabilities of how AI could serve as a tool to achieve better realities for ourselves and members of our communities? I vote for the latter but this is not a foregone conclusion as currently most use cases of artificial intelligence are commandeered by billion-dollar corporations optimizing and monetizing our awareness or governments scaling AI to keep an eye on us.

But what would be possible if the potential of AI were available to smaller teams, communities, or even individuals to create solutions to tap into the scope of human potential? Let's face it, what are the chances a billion-dollar corporation would utilize AI to tackle issues outside their specific interests? Yes, there are exceptions but I believe smaller communities of developers building out AI solutions for the communities they work in will root to the core interests of the people more than institutional solutions alone. At least this would be an arrow in the quiver of utilizing AI to tap into human potential.

Decentralized AI is not a singular mission but Ben Goertzel with Singularitynet.io seems to be leading the charge with the concept of a toolset to carry decentralized AI forward. Their team certainly seems to be on an interesting track where they provide a framework for even the smallest developers to harness the potential of AI. I just don't see how a world I envisioned through the lens of The Emergence moves forward without the assistance of AI as we are all naturally limited in our ability to acquire awareness and context so how do we navigate this increasingly noisy world we live in if we are not aware and do not have the right toolset to render context for ourselves.

Indeed we could disappear into the woods and live off the grid until our dying days (which is certainly an option) but for those of us who continue to stay in the grind, we are surrounded by AI making decisions for us every waking minute. What happens when AI begins to make more decisions for us than we make four ourselves? So do we fight AI or fight for AI to be under our control and to serve our best interests? This is what Singuarlitynet seems to be working on and is something our technology companies, our legislators, and the people should be fighting for.

Whether it is Singularity Net, the Solid framework, the Ethereum blockchain, GunDB, or any other framework that can be imagined to secure and engage the interests and minds of the users, as soon as these frameworks become more important than the people they serve, we are back to square one. As soon as frameworks become an opportunity for shareholders' interests over the interests of the stakeholders, we're back to the status quo.

I am hopeful though. Although there has always been pent up frustration with the status quo regardless of the era of humanity, now seems different. Now frameworks are on the horizon to help engage people at their core. To increase understanding and capabilities beyond what social orders deem necessary to what is innate within each of us. This feels like the mid 90's where hope ran rampant from what seemed possible with the world wide web.

This time it is my sincerest desire, we learn from history to not repeat the same mistakes as I am not sure how many do-overs we have before technology enables us to no longer have our hands on the wheel rendering experiences. Some might ask why we need an open framework, to begin with, and to just let humans figure it out. My response is that the cat is out of the bag, so it is better to try to move these tools under user control before it is too late.

Yes, we could rely on the free market to solve these problems through Adam Smith's invisible hand but I fundamentally believe he didn't foresee the weight of corporate influence in the exchange we see today. Finding a set of frameworks for applications to help balance the interests of users, businesses, and governments is a tall order but necessary for the long term growth and health of societal interests. Should these frameworks be private or public entities are incredibly difficult questions to answer.

I for one believe these frameworks should at least be a mixture of employee and community-owned interests with financial and operational transparency at the very core of their operations. Without this, we require the trust of those with influence to do the right thing. Trust is either assumptive or verifiable. I for one believe the latter speaks better to the public's interest.

And this leads me to.......

Number Four: The Application Layer

The main reason I am so hopeful though is what is at the heart of The Emergence which is the application layer built on top of a decentralized connection to move user experiences away from the control of the network and the providers attached to it. Applications are rendered through smart phones, computers, TVs, smart watches, kiosks, IoT devices, and in the future through smart glasses. dApps or decentralized applications are a style of application arriving on the scene utilizing the Blockchain or a peer-to-peer framework but the term to me should extend beyond blockchain to include any type of application built to engage user data outside centralized control.

If Solid takes off as a domain-based framework, shouldn't the apps be considered decentralized if they are outside the control of the network? At least, I believe so. But as stated above just because an application is decentralized does not mean it will empower the user. Without legislation to set and enforce the laws and decentralized frameworks in place to manage user data without fear of influence, I fear decentralized applications will have more bark than bite.

But even with laws and open frameworks in place, just because an app is outside the control of the network or the providers doesn't necessarily mean the app is reaching into the depths of human potential. Decentralization is the baseline to protect and secure user data from the threats of outside control and manipulation but where the true potential lies is when applications are both decentralized and purposeful for the user and the communities they are engaged with. Technology to inspire purpose throughout society might sound like social engineering but as opposed to society being engineered from the top as is currently the case, society would be engineered through a toolset under the control of the people from within society.

A fundamental idea at the core of how I see the Emergence and what made the lightbulb go off in my head at the bookstore. Just like ant colonies, what are the signals between people, goods, and services best able to protect and allow people to thrive within the communities they not only live in but engage with? Could a decentralized and purposeful application layer be the carrier of these signals? I believe so and for ease and the benefit of this podcast moving forward I will refer to this form of application as an emergent application. Admittedly, a bit self-serving but also to the point.

Let me change the perspective for a bit. Do YOU want to emerge from where you are in society? I don't care if it relates to your family, your friends, your work, your team, your government, or your gang? I don't care if you are a CEO or homeless. A woman, man, or non-binary. Black, white, brown. Theist or atheist, Does society exercise your true potential? I'm not talking about only your financial potential but your human potential. Is society protecting your interests and encouraging your interests and capabilities to best serve yourself and your communities? Should it?

Those on the right will say this is not the role of society and should be up to the individual to emerge, especially in a free market based democratic society where seizing the opportunity is at the core of exercising one's potential. Those on the left will say it is the fundamental role of government within society to meet the needs of the represented. To those on the right, I ask should the ideal of life, liberty, and the pursuit of happiness be limited to only the resilient? If so, doesn't this provide a firmament for powerful governmental and business interests to exert controls over the populace?

To those on the left, I ask if meeting the needs of the people is more important than providing tools for them to seize opportunities, doesn't this provide firmament for powerful government interests to exert controls over the populace? I think history can prove societal extremes from either the left or right ends up with the overall health of represented societies suffering.

I personally believe free markets are the better firmament for societal health than Marxist utopian dreams but I also believe free markets are leaving way too many people on the sidelines. This is something I've never understood when you see cities overrun with homelessness and crime. How does blame contribute to the overall health of a city? How does the militarization of policing that started with the 1997 1033 program to transfer military arms to local police departments contribute to social order? [4] Is this model working out for us? Is the solution a heavier hand? To bring in national forces to clean the streets of the homeless and the destroyers of property to stamp down unrest and distress.

Maybe this would have been an effective strategy in an unconnected world as in the past but I don't see things playing out as they had in the past since we are now living in a world where an application layer optimized for monetary value over human value serves as an instigator of the human condition. Serving as a beacon to entice and distract more than invite and engage. The pick yourself up by your bootstraps model for success is not working. The blame game is not working. And the rioting is not working.

We are divided, while connected like no other time in history, through tools we are not in control of, offering the marginalized a soapbox full of dynamite. And as automation continues to replace unskilled workers, the cost of acquiring skills continues to increase exponentially, and long-established societal norms are being challenged daily, somebody was bound to light the fuse.

Did we really not see this coming? But It is my fundamental belief that if the application layer were optimized for human value over monetary value, business and governments would find friends they didn't realize they had by inspiring an engaged populace more than an enraged one.

This would be a good time to articulate that I admit I am a bit out of my depth here. I'm not a scholar with the right connections. And to be brutally honest I don't have an innate desire to be liked by the very people who could help build this future. I mean seriously I'm asking for complete financial transparency from the frameworks that could help build this future. Do you think I will be invited to all the great parties? No..... my role in all of this will be to ask the more difficult questions that someone with a career or ideology to protect may not ask? I actually see my lack of credentials as a plus in this quest and truly intend on being the grain of sand in the eye of the status quo whichever side of the political spectrum it sees from.

I promise you, I don't pretend to have all the answers and have absolutely no problem being called out on my lack of research or depth of study. I see well-positioned disagreement as an amazing opportunity to learn and grow from and it is my greatest desire that communication tools in the future harness the power of disagreement as fuel for the birth of solutions over the festering of problems.

So in service of what could be the emergent application layer, I would like to ask two simple questions. Should everybody regardless of their income level, race, religion, or gender status have the same opportunity to exercise their potential to help themselves and the communities they interact with? If they do not, what is possible when barriers limiting this potential begin to fall?

I do not come at these questions lightly either, I assure you, because the notion of barriers holding back human potential is at the center of the political storm we are in. Barriers limiting potential based on income levels, race, gender, and mental and physical capacity from the perspective of the left are clearly much higher than those of the right, so where is the solution when our political will is so divided? I set out on a mission early on in the development of this podcast to speak to both the right and the left and to not exclude non-extreme elements of either side. A tall order for the world we live in.

Personally, I was raised in a very loving and non-judgemental republican family with a dad and mom who voted for Truman, Kennedy, and then Reagan as the democratic party started to move further to the left. Other than a wonderful sister who is a liberal, the rest of my family and most of my friends growing up leaned more to the right, so I have always been surrounded by people I love who happened to be on the right side of the political spectrum. But I have always been torn between the promise of the free market providing opportunities for all and the realities that have come to bear. But on the other hand, I'm also aware of what happens when the pendulum swings too far to the other side when governments flatten the reward of effort and seize control in the name of the people.

What is sacrificed when these barriers are lowered? The conservatives will argue, our freedom, job creation, cultural integrity, and national security. What is sacrificed if these barriers are not lowered? The liberals and the left will say equality of opportunity, cultural diversity, and freedom of choice.

How far America has come but how far it still has to go without sacrificing the engine behind progress is certainly a tall order. Do we rely on government and business to determine the size of these barriers? Is this the only plan for progress? For parties of government to agree on who deserves what. For big business to favor shareholder value over stakeholder interests as a model for progress?

Believe me, I realize I am baking this down into a very easy digestible cake so this is wildly more complicated than this but I believe true progress should be at the feet of the people as much as any business or the government. What if the people had better tools at their disposal to engage without a threat of outside influence, to push government and business to become more effective in service of their interests rather than the other way around.

Without a doubt business and government play a significant role in progress but I truly feel we have become too reliant solely on their good behavior. Couldn't it be argued, tapping into the interest and capabilities of those who do and could work in these spaces would help render better systems? And by reducing barriers for all of society to participate within these systems wouldn't this end up benefiting society as a whole?

So what is possible when an emergent application layer focuses on increasing creativity, awareness, productivity, and empathy amongst all people who do and could work within systems of business, government, and social engagement. Not something achievable overnight but as a larger arc in human development, what could be achieved when a baseline of emergent applications are made available as more of a social utility than only a commercial transaction. A social utility to strengthen the market from the bottom up through purposeful applications engaging workers, managers, owners, philanthropists, and most importantly members of society not able or willing to contribute.

Barriers can either be lowered through system pressure or levers could be built to raise those who are blocked by internal or external forces. Emergent applications would be a form of lever, to help people emerge from behavioral and environmental limitations found within the human condition. Think of nodes in a system. The more resilient the nodes, the stronger the system. To date, a lack of a resonant connection has allowed systems of government and business too much control over outcomes making a stronger shell but weaker core. A shell largely being eaten away by division aggravated by a noisy connection.

But opportunities exist today to reduce this noise and strengthen the core by providing a spade for people to dig for what moves them the most to either climb over or remove barriers in the way of societal progress. Progress coming from people as much as systems composed of people. Without a doubt systems are important but when people inside and outside of systems are more effectively harnessing their potential, everybody would benefit.

So what would an emergent application look like? There really is no end to a list of apps that could speak to the promise of tapping into human potential which I will delve into on future episodes but for the purposes of this intro, I'll focus on one area of interest for the application layer which is through the lens of mental health as I had spoken of earlier.

To me, mental health is at the very root of societal ills we see today and in the eyes of the emergence, covers a large spectrum of the human condition from the most severe cases of schizophrenia to mild cases of anxiety and levels of frustration in how we handle experiences surrounding us both near and far. States of mind affecting decisions made by the homeless, criminals, the military, the police, CEO's, welfare mothers, doctors, or kids tempted to join a gang.

How many times has your mental state negatively affected the way you handled a situation at work, at home, on the field, or in your profession? Now add externalities such as the environment you are in, other internal conflicts, and 24/7 information overload and it is not hard to see how altered mental states can manifest into frustration, bad behaviors, misunderstandings, and missed opportunities.

Criminal activity, homelessness, police brutality, toxic work environments, drug abuse, sexual abuse, racism, etc., etc. How much of a factor does mental health play in all of this

when in the U.S alone, close to 50% of the population has
suffered some form of mental illness much less traumatic
mental conditions such as anxiety or depression not classified
as an illness? Not to give systems of governance and
business a pass for the existence of barriers but internal
barriers within people may also be holding people back since
it is easy to argue unhealthy people are responsible for
unhealthy systems.

How much of a cost to society does this reality bear? Wouldn't
an increase in the quality of mental health across society
decrease criminal behavior and homelessness and improve
parenting skills, leadership skills, and interpersonal
relationships? Certainly not a quick fix but over time I believe
a moonshot on mental health could create an environment to
help improve the human condition. I imagine most people are
interested in a healthier society but some are concerned with
what may be sacrificed in its pursuit when institutions are the
primary means of moving the needle.

And I believe tackling mental health through the lens of
emergent applications could be a bipartisan approach to
move the needle on mental health. Tools provided to all
people to improve their mental health to positively impact their
lives, the lives of their loved ones, the communities they
engage with, and systems of business and government they
interact with.

Notice how I focus on mental health over mental illness as I
believe this is something we could all benefit from. Certainly, I
don't blame the current state of mental health squarely on the
shoulders of a highly centralized communication technology
model wrapped around an institutionalized framework for

mental health but I do believe they carry a significant portion of the burden in missing opportunities for social progress.

Granted, I come from this from a 40,000-foot view and would love to dig into this topic with people in the know on future episodes but for this introductory episode, I would like to inspire a debate around what would be possible with a decentralized, community-based approach utilizing communication technology to help people understand and relate to what is inside and outside of who they are. When the mind is healthy, the body will follow so I see emergent applications serving a broad-spectrum of engagement to include therapy, training, and information discovery.

Training and Therapy Applications

Let's take training and therapy to start with to layout ideas behind emergent applications used in the context of mental health. I would like to use the George Floyd murder as a lens to see the potential of these types of applications through. The ex-Navy seal Jocko Willink talks about the importance of situational training in the military to deescalate potential hostile situations. He mentioned in a Joe Rogan podcast how this always-on mode of situational training should be a staple of the American police force but that it is not.

Training to condition new recruits as well as established veterans in the endless cascade of changing situations they have to deal with every day of their professional lives. It is interesting to note that according to the National Conference of State Legislatures only 20 states currently require mental health training for police departments.

Of these 20 states, who decide the training protocols, the technology to use, the contractors to implement the technology, the frequency of the training, and most importantly how to measure the effectiveness of the adoption and retention of use. How engaged are the stakeholders who are the members of the communities and the officers in this process? How would all of this translate into better mental health?

Awareness and understanding are at the very center of mental health as when we are put into situations we are not prepared for, negative outcomes have a better chance of surfacing creating environments for anxiety and depression to flourish shutting down reason as a tool to cope with. I am neither a psychiatrist nor a psychologist but I can talk from personal experience when I am put in the situations I am not prepared for and something bad happens, how I handle the situation can have repercussions negatively affecting my reality.

So in the George Floyd murder could different training protocols have rendered different outcomes? Now I am not aware of the training protocols leading to both scenarios and I have never served as a police officer or in the military so my perspective is skewed. You could say I have not lived in the shoes of the officers during these situations but on the other hand, most officers have not lived in the shoes of those they engage with to protect the communities they serve.

But despite my ignorance of the specifics, I wonder if there are opportunities to use emergent applications to increase awareness and understanding of police officers with the situations inherent within the communities they serve. To better relate to conditions on the ground to proactively engage rather than reactively enforce.

Maybe these technologies already exist, I don't know, but I would like to partly use this podcast as a vehicle to find out how communication technologies are used to help police forces build better relationships with the communities they are paid by tax dollars to serve and protect. Not to attack those who serve but to better understand how their systems are supporting the members of their forces in this quest. To ask questions on how they are sourcing, modifying, and personalizing such technology and how involved the stakeholders are in the process.

Where training is to prepare mental states for what is to come, therapy helps mental states cope with the past. How could emergent applications help those suffering from past experiences cope with the world they live in? There are countless mental therapy apps out there but the idea behind the emergence is to focus on those applications and future applications that are not controlled by any interest outside that of the end-user and their communities.

What do I mean? If an application is flooded with non-relevant and distracting advertising to the user this is non-emergent. If the application is funded with an agenda to drive sales or increase a user base from a Big Pharma company, institution, or an association, this is non-emergent. If the application collects user data and re-purposes it for anything other than the specific interests of the user, this is non-emergent.

An Emergent application for mental therapy would be one that engages the user at a visceral level to help shore up their emotional core so the intellectual is not stifled. The problem with conventional centralized technology is that to understand the emotional layer, personal information has to be mined which could be used to influence future behavior or to be monetized outside the interest of the user.

But what is possible when trust is gained and the user is able to use technology to help explore their mental state through the alignment of those who could relate and through available resources? To help dig deep within but also to connect resonantly with others to help identify counseling, therapy, homeopathic, and medicinal remedies. Imagine finding someone who "gets you" but also has the background to help you beyond merely words.

Let me go back to the George Floyd case. He was found with high levels of fentanyl in his system and he had a criminal record. I have heard some use this as an excuse for what led to the outcome of the situation he was in. First of all, there is just no justification for a knee on the neck of a handcuffed human being regardless of their state of mind or their crime for that matter.

That is a baseline. Now add in the nuance of the color of his skin with his state of mind and how he may have perceived the situation. I hear this all the time, just comply with the police and everything will be OK. Truth be told, I would. Without a doubt, I would smother the police with kindness. That is how I was raised and even if I was impaired, odds are I would be even nicer.

But I haven't lived in George Floyd's shoes. I imagine I wouldn't see the police the same way he did even if I tried. I understand I live in a different environment than he did so I am unable to naturally relate to his perspective, just as I can't relate to the experiences of women, transgenders, or those suffering from extreme poverty. But just because I can't relate does not mean I need to judge in the vacuum of understanding? I believe if George Floyd had access to people and resources to help him cope with his realities at the same time police officers were helped in better understanding the perceptions of members of his community, progress might have a chance.

I fully realize I am trying to distill this incredibly complicated and difficult topic into a few soundbites for a podcast intro but I sincerely believe technology has a role to play in bridging this divide and in future episodes would like to engage with the members of the police and minority communities to help identify methodologies and technologies that are being used successfully in some communities but not in others. Or possibly to find methodologies and technologies used in other industries successfully that could be used to help bridge the divide between police enforcement and the communities they serve.

What other areas in the sphere of mental health could Emergent Applications benefit? From homelessness to workplace productivity, familial relationships, extremism, and racism; the possibilities are endless when applications are identified and built to provide a secure and purposeful environment for the user to reach within and outside to those who relate the most to their potential and the unique situations they are in. Suicide rates in the U.S have increased 35% over the last 20 years according to a new report from the U.S. Centers for Disease Control and Prevention, which is beyond troubling when you realize the highest growth rate for suicides is with young adults.

People need to have goals. People need to have a purpose to keep moving them forward. When they feel lost whether it is due to an extreme case of mental illness or just feeling shut out from the rest of the world, their potential is stifled which can and will affect opportunities taken. Add to this, the 24/7 noise-making machine we call the media preying on the most basic of our instincts it is no wonder we are where we are.

When our mental health is compromised, we are easily distracted and easily influenced to make decisions both monetarily and personally that are counter to our self-interests. What would it look like if our experiences were not in the hands of billion-dollar media companies and trillion-dollar technology companies and applications were optimized for our mental health more than just our pocketbooks? That is a conversation to have for future episodes.

Collaboration Applications

Back in the 1960s and 70's the inventor of the computer mouse and the brain behind the Mother of all Demos, Douglas Englebart, began to build a pre-internet computer network to allow users to collaborate on information they consumed, created, and shared. His vision of his NLS or oN-Line System was in many ways a precursor to the internet we see today but also a lesson in what was missed in how the internet has evolved. One feature set missed In today's iteration of the web is that of collaboration being baked Into the DNA of the user experience. You can see it in his mother of all demos presented in 1968 where Douglas and his team remotely collaborated on a shared document in real-time which is linked to in the podcast notes.

Yes, cloud-based documents and certain applications invite collaboration but web pages are not collaborative by nature limiting the scalability of people working together. What would be possible if the entire ecosystem of the web was collaborative by default to engage the potential of ideas and feedback between users and resources on the web, moving users outside the confines of silos to experience expanded feature sets?

For instance, imagine logging into an art gallery website where you are joined by an art historian who is also logged in to discuss the history of a piece displayed on the site. All of the links, resources, and comments shared around this piece would be viewable on the site as well as could be moved to another site featuring a seminar based on the topic of the piece in question that could also be moved to a shared calendar item for an upcoming artist appearance. All the while carrying the link back to the original artwork to inspire a sale organically outside the confines of the original retail web view.

If you can't tell by now, The Emergence I/O is not steeped in short term gain from small ideas but the long term potential of big ideas to bring people together through the connection. Something I believe will pay off in spades to society when applications reach beyond the attention heavy model we see today optimized for monetary gain only. How could this be achieved? By using collaboration as more of a universal standard to follow rather than an individual feature set made available from a provider. A notion representative of the battle for the web where open standards for web pages to follow are pitted against features made available through siloed applications monetized for user engagement.

To my understanding, this is the path the Solid Framework is on in addition to creating secure data environments for users where applications and web pages built to their framework standards would allow for open and secure exchanges of information between users, applications, and pages involved. Think about the spacing of bolts on a hub for a tire rim.

There's a universal standard that all manufactures of rims follow to help companies effectively create customized rims to fit on vehicles, effectively allowing vendors to collaborate to create an end product to help people move from point a to point b. Imagine if each vendor and each company involved were allowed to create their own spacing to help create more of an exclusive offering, wouldn't this impede the end-user from getting from point a to point b, whether through inconvenience or cost?

Embracing standards to encourage open source development to promote a frictionless exchange and collaboration between what is created, consumed, and shared amongst users is at the very core of The Emergence. I believe it will be the developers who will be the most important links in this chain as they will be the ones to adopt and push these standards to the market. Without these standards, an open ecosystem of collaborative emergent applications is just a pipe dream but who will carry this out?

Tim Berners Lee is the director of the W3C commission who is in charge of web standards as well as heads up the solid framework so it seems to reason Solid is positioned well for this role. Will app and web devs begin to embrace this or will they continue to build rims with different spacing for bolts. Certainly not the Devs fault if they do – because I'm not sure what type of incentive they would have to do otherwise.

From what I have experienced in my research and participation in this space this very question is at the heart of the future of the web. Is the overall arc of the future web for the benefit of commercial interests or for the public good? Of course, it will be a mixture of both but which one will be the dominant force? If we stay with the status quo it is easy to see which side will be favored.

Information Discovery Applications

This one is my obsession. What could an emergent application layer bring to information discovery among the connected? To help bring people deeper into experiences. To allow them to easily verify the authenticity of authorship and trustworthiness of the content discovered. To allow the user to reach deep inside their interests and situations to reveal content that speaks to them viscerally and intellectually. To align user interests with other users based on their professional, academic, or personal backgrounds to reveal experiences that resonate more fully within the exchange.

To blend the real world with the digital world through immersive technologies such as VR, AR, and Spatial computing to engage users with objects and situations like no other time in the history of the human experience. To empower users with tools to be influential over their means of discovery to be challenged and to challenge to grow their understanding of the world around them.

Unfortunately, this is not the web as we know it. Maybe in pockets of applications but users are far from influential over their own experiences on the greater web. By and large, they are servants to it, becoming more of a product to be monetized than individuals to be purposefully engaged with.

Something that has been brilliantly unpacked in the recent Netflix documentary, The Social Dilemma where a host of insiders warn how Google, Facebook, Twitter, and other big tech players are creating technology to trigger addictive dopamine rushes in users, mine user attention for profit, and socially engineer user behavior through manipulation and persuasion. The web it argues is treating humans as a commodity by digging deep into their brain stems to prey on their most basic instincts to influence consumption.

I think it is a fair argument when you look at the paucity of tools to help users condition their feeds of information there is no surprise in what is filling the void. From predictive text forming thoughts, to analyzing behaviors to influence future ones best suited to the needs of providers, to the removal of information contrary to common understanding; information has become a powerful tool for authority over thought rather than tools for deep inquiry and engagement.

Add onto this a mind-numbing media complex barraging users with duplicative content harvested through bots, ad networks flooding our senses with non-relevance and interruptions, and news feeds trolling for the lowest common denominator through headline baiting and one has to wonder where this will lead within the next 5 years.

To me, the future is dire if efforts are not made to reverse these trends. And I believe it lies more at the feet of the application layer than anything else. Specifically, with discovery tools. Build it purposefully and they will come in kind should be the motto for the future of the web. Although I enjoyed the Social Dilemma, I have to admit I was let down a bit by the abundance of problems identified without many solutions offered.

One solution offered in the documentary was for people to leave social altogether but I believe the social connection has the potential to be inspiring and deeply resonant if it were in the hands of the people. Same thing with search and other methods of discovery but to be candid I don't see toolsets rendered by multi-billion dollar corporations such as Facebook, Twitter, or Google making significant changes to empower users. That ship has sailed. Big will never go back to small in my opinion. They probably couldn't if they tried as there is so much pressure from shareholders to deliver perpetual growth which will always be at the expense of quality engagement for the user.

No, I believe the path forward is to build an endless supply of smaller applications built on open and secure standards to allow people to connect and exchange experiences outside the control of silos and providers. Actually, more reminiscent of how the web was originally built. How would this be possible when big tech has such a stronghold on users? I believe it will have to come from users and developers pushing the creation of applications outside the control of providers and the network to inspire better frameworks and legislation to come from these efforts. A bottom-up approach to effectively build better systems from the efforts of the people.

And I feel information discovery tools should be at the heart of this movement to build better tools to engage the potential of the connection rather than manipulate it.

How to affect this change?

By encouraging high school labs and college computer science departments to experiment with new ways for users to discover and share experiences outside the influence of networks and providers. To help find purpose within the connection. Facebook was founded out of a Harvard dorm room. Imagine the possibilities if resources were applied to the innovative potential of learners within collaborative environments built around the ideas of user empowerment.

By creating grant programs to inspire developers and innovative thinkers to build applications at the community level to help members of the communities to discover resources, interact with legislation affecting the communities, and engage with those entrusted with growing and protecting their communities.

By harnessing social impact funds and philanthropic funding to create an ecosystem of social applications to make available for free and without ads as a public utility to help bring people together to share ideas, access resources, and encourage learning.

By incentivizing businesses through tax breaks and subsidies to use or build emergent applications to empower their workforce, management teams, and potential hires around the notion of aligning individual interests and capabilities with opportunities. Not through top-down directives to maximize profits but from within to explore the true potential of labor,

What would emergent discovery applications look like? At the core would be alignment or a word I've been using quite frequently which is Tuning. To reach deep inside oneself to articulate and dig for interests and situations then tune these to information, products, services, situations, and even objects found through VR/AR found through the connection. Mind you this only works in a decentralized and secure connection since the last thing anyone would want to do is share their innermost interests and situations in the connection only to be harvested and manipulated by government and business concerns.

This is the reason it is so important to separate our data from the application and to flip the narrative of the user logging into a service to a service asking permission to access the user's data. A role reversal that would seed unlimited user potential for discovery throughout the connection. What could users tune to their interests and situations when these roles are reversed. Here are a few ideas.

Civically, users could align their interests, situations, and feedback with pending legislation, policies, and procedures happening within their communities affecting their livelihood, well-being, and access to opportunities. Instances currently hidden behind walls of file formats, bureaucracy, and political proxies that when liberated could increase the buy-in of the electorate while decreasing dissonance.

Professionally, users could align their interests and situations with opportunities within the marketplace beyond the confines of traditional administrative roles and conventional work silos reaching deep inside the dynamics and personalities involved with the opportunity to surface unrealized capabilities.

Socially, users could align their interests and situations with others to discover character traits, shared experiences, interests, and passions to transcend beyond the binary world of agreement versus disagreement the social connection delivers today.

Commercially, users could align their interests and situations with products, services, and situations to move beyond merely a transaction to a measure of trust and engagement with brands to meet the needs and desires of the user. I always say it is not advertising if you are interested. The state of advertising on the web is a lazy layer of behavior manipulation technology slapped on top of a 100-year-old Madison Avenue model. There are a host of innovative companies out there looking to evolve this space, so I am looking forward to having conversations with those who see value in the interests of the users as much as the providers.

Personally, users could align their interests and situations with information, entertainment. and news from sources to relate to and inspire deeper levels of engagement and inquiry. Currently, engagement is treated as more of a monetization strategy where algorithms condition relevance of discovery for the benefit of the provider but what would be possible when discovery would be conditioned for what lies deep inside the user without fear of outside influence. Not to discover what is popular on the outside but what resonates from within. Not to be fed what is divisive but invited to what stimulates understanding whether one agrees or not.

To have a trust mechanism built into the DNA of every discovery tool allowing the user to easily view sources and flags to alert for potential inconsistencies found in the content. To be able to tune what is read, listened to, or watched based on what lies within the content and the background, profession, education. or interests of the author.

But not only what one brings in to shape inquiry but what is offered back in feedback to shape engagement. In an emergent application, feedback would be baked into the discovery process beyond comments and rating of only the quality of the content but the quality of the experience overall. Was the content informative? Was it trustworthy? Were there passages that resonated more than others? Did the content lead to a positive action? Not metadata for outside interests to influence future behaviors but metadata to help future discovery and if specific permissions were granted to help authors or services improve the quality of content and services offered.

I have recently been digging into the theory of Cybernetics on building better systems and realized a similarity in what I am talking about in their theory with the importance of feedback in building better systems. If this is broken down to its very core, the quality of the feedback we give back to systems of business, government, and social will determine the health of the related systems. But feedback is highly influenced by the input received. Increase the quality of the input and quality output will follow which will help define better systems.

Of course, there are many variables involved with this but giving people the ability to tune their input and output based on what motivates them will bring more purpose into the system. Especially when tools are in place to allow reward to be exchanged in the effort. Whether the reward is validation of effort, monetary compensation, a fulfilling experience, or the satisfaction of helping another, the potential of the connection lies within the quality of this exchange.

Discovery is at the core of The Emergence because when we discover and share resonantly, we are carrying this forward for the discovery of others in the systems. What could a resonant system of discovery do in the areas of government, business, and social interactions? The sky's the limit.

If this sounds like a bit more work than the passive feed culture we live in, it is. But easy and quick in the hyper-connected world we live in is proving to only amplify the worst of what resides in all of us already. Our thoughts are now a product and engineered to maximize profits and we are only in the beginning phase if something is not done to reverse the course we are on.

The early days of these new tools may require a bit more work from the user but over time will become more intuitive if the willpower is there to take this on. I am hoping the work with the solid framework, Singualritynet, and Etherium to name a few will inspire the building of these tools but it will be the innovative spirit of the devs and idea smiths who will be the ones who push this future forward. To completely rethink the purpose of information as more of a tool wielded by people to build better societies rather than tools for societies to build better people.

One of my biggest complaints about communication technologies outside of control issues is the amount of friction that remains within the exchange. I have been saying this for years and will continue to shout about it. What is the difference between an email, a text, a word doc, a video file, an audio file, or a dataset? Absolutely nothing if you treat them all as instances within experiences to create, consume, and share.

Vannevar Bush theorized about this in 1948 with his essay, As We May Think where he describes a future memex machine creating trails of experiences for users to create and follow. Fast forward 70 years and we have not built trails to discover experiences on our own accord and thoughtfully but highways to deliver us to destinations predictively and expeditiously. In the future, experiences should be seen as connecting user's trails of instances within experiences by phone number, email address, or web id, removing the middlemen of relevance connecting the specifics over the generalities of life.

I'd like to do a little thought experiment on this to help work through this concept. Imagine you're on a hike when you come across hieroglyphics on a rock that intrigues you. You take a picture that is stored in your personal vault or maybe in the future your solid POD. From within your vault without logging into any other service, you text the photo to a friend who comments she knows a professor of linguistics who could help translate the symbols into text. This comment would be stored in the friend's vault but would be embedded in yours which would be attached to the photo. Both the photo and comment would exist as a shared experience accessible only to the owners of the respective vaults.

Now the friend invites the professor into the shared experience through their web I.D. who adds snippets of text from a public vault and a private vault both carrying a link back to the source material as well as the professor's translation. You then decide to make this shared experience public and proceed to email potentially interested friends from within your vault to invite them to add commentary and resources.

Since the shared experience is set to public, algorithms on the decentralized web crawl the metadata of the shared experience for level of engagement and the backgrounds of the participants whose profiles are set to public to help others on the web discover an experience born from the real world supplemented by the digital. After a while you decide the application facilitating the shared experience lacks in feature sets so you decide to move the entire experience over to a new provider who offers fact-checking, a customized AI to inspire deeper engagement, a tunable ad model to each user experience to raise money for the park where the hieroglyphic was discovered, and a better UI. All the while your data and that of your collaborators stays in their personal vaults.

As you may notice, within this entire thought experiment, absolutely no data is shared outside the explicit interests of the participants. I might be off on some of the specifics in what could be rendered but the concept is possible and is necessary if we want to dig to find what resides inside the best of us. To create more of an emergent network than a social network to engage the potential of the users. Something personal, securable, and scalable to help resonate the potential of people into systems of business, government, and social.

Currently, our instances are stored in the vaults of corporations and governments where when we log in to their silos, we ask for their permission to use our experiences, and by default give them ownership. Better yet they also tell us how we should discover and use our instances and that of others based on algorithms used on our behalf. It is literally like living in a car driven by a complete stranger who is paid by a corporation to take us where they want us to go. Yes, we can get out at any time we want as long as we are willing to walk.

These cars storing our experiences are made of components only accessible to the largest corporations to drive our future forward. Whether it is a word doc, spreadsheet, and increasingly the web or any other means of communication provisioned by big tech, they have the keys and we are the passengers. As Marshal McLuhan said in the 1960s, the medium is the message which has ended up incredibly prophetic. But the messages within the exchange, which are a collection of our experiences, are more influenced by the mediums of TV, Radio, Print, and the web than what Marshall McLuhan could have ever imagined because now the connection is two way, 24/7, and real-time. An environment ripe for manipulation when we are not in control of the toolset and the algorithms feeding our realities. Big tech and big media have built an ecosystem where how they sell us is becoming more important than what they are selling us, where the value of distraction has trumped the value of deep engagement.

What If The Status Quo

As I reflect back with my new emergent lens, in the early days of the web, I would have had reason to be hopeful this toolset I describe would already be here. We had open blogs, RSS feeds, podcasts, and comments managed through an open connection. It wasn't perfect but it was ripe with possibilities to scale to at least a modicum of the future I wished for.

Who am I to envision such a future? Absolutely nobody. Which is the point. This web wasn't going to be built for the movers and the shakers. This web was going to be built for the muckrakers, the engagers, and the dreamers. Those who wanted to be a part of something greater than just building another firmament to extract value from the few but a firmament to bring value to all. In a potentially emergent world, the early web was a model to mix the ideals of social progress with the innovative forces of a free market but then web 2.0 put the brakes on this dream as our experiences were cordoned off into silos and the connection became a noisy marketplace optimized for monetary value over human value.

What happens if we don't correct the path we're on? Where a handful of media and technology companies render relevance and interests to the connected. Where one day these centrally-controlled experiences will be rendered through our smart glasses, literally surrounding our perception of the world with what best serves the market.

I fondly remember showing friends my PDA back in the late '90s and wondering what it would be like when we would be connected to the internet through these devices. Too many times I was met with - why would we need to be connected through a mobile device when a computer was nearby to connect?. Not a judgment call at all. Back then, this type of tech was the fodder of nerds but just as many felt they would never need to connect through a mobile device, many today will say they will never wear glasses.

I am going to call it now. Within 10 years, smart glasses will be the smartphone of today. There will just be too many potential uses for users to pass on. But in my opinion, this could render a concerning reality if we continue the path we are on by giving up the experiences we create, consume, and share to the network and to the providers.

History

Before communication technology, those in power had a tight rein on the signal of the human voice to influence the community in the direction of their choosing. Enter the printing press, telegraph, telephone, radio, and TV amplifying the signal between people yet still influencing society from the top down to include Hitler and Goebbels subsidizing Volksempfanger radio sets to spread Nazi propaganda throughout the German republic,, Rwanda radio explicitly calling for the extermination of the Tutsi ethnic group,, and William Randolph Hearst manufacturing stories in Cuba through his newspaper to fan the flames for a Spanish American war.

Over time, the transmission of information became another form of weapon molding knowledge and understanding within the rank and file of society as a means of control. Centers of power-wielding perception over the masses like a sword to instill fear, confusion, and allegiance to the ruling party while withholding and manipulating context.

Today we see certain levels of this where information is manipulated to not only preserve power but to push interests with the carrot of convenience to consumers defining how we work and what we are worth. Mass consumerism fueled by a connection conditioning our signal strength while ushering in an era defined by quantity over quality and reaction over clarity. Signals exchanged reaching far but not deep.

I truly believe the overall thread of communication technology plays off our lowest common denominator rather than the highest, serving to divide more than inspire. To incite and excite more than invite. An exchange of value favoring monetary gains over personal efforts losing sight of the true potential of the connection.

We Are Divided

The human condition is such that we have always been divided to some degree but there seems to be something in the air that is different now. Something exponential about how the connection is now and what could come from it without a fundamental shift in how it is delivered. As I discussed earlier, we have the toolset to unite more than divide, yet these tools are under the control of institutions rather than people to render their own better realities.

Everything we discover through the web, the results are chosen for us. Even when we search, an algorithm filters the results primarily based on the popularity of the content and relevance based on our implicit behaviors rather than our explicit actions. When we are on social media, the comments we see from friends are chosen for us. When we watch historic events unfold, the original content disappears into a menagerie of talking heads, each with a point of view to mold our perspective like potter's clay.

A perfect example of this is the first interview between Joe Rogan and Elon musk which I personally found incredibly interesting as there were a number of subjects covered such as artificial intelligence, driverless technology, and green technology that spoke to my core interests. But when I returned to search for the episode to rewatch a certain section, my results were filled with clips of commentary talking about Elon Musk smoking a joint.

Certainly an accurate depiction of what happened, yet far from what I found relevant from within the dialogue. Actually, for the first couple of days after the episode hit the web, I couldn't find the original source on the first page when I searched for the keywords Joe Rogan Elon Musk podcast. What was revealed was just a cascading list of commentary on Elon musk smoking a joint from all the top news sites.

Fast forward to the horrific murder of George Floyd by the police where I attempted to share an unedited video of the incident with a friend to help explain the gravity of the situation without a narrative but was met with an endless stream of videos with reactions and proclamations spliced into the footage instead. Vignettes of experiences out of my control on the web serving as kindling for the fire that was about to erupt, moving the very real and wildly important movement of the protesters into the chaos that would ensue.

Chaos feeding off media and tech companies amplifying and filtering the signal to surface blame and anger between the right and the left. No, I am not excusing the actions of the rioters but I do understand where the anger is coming from and see a significant role the media and big tech are playing in fanning the literal flames.

We ALL have this amazing opportunity to engage and learn yet we are stifled by the noise. We ALL have this amazing opportunity to bring our brothers and sisters from our communities into the fold, yet we are distracted and divided. We are frustrated and I would imagine far more of the connected feel marginalized as they compare themselves to the real-time Joneses or are so overwhelmed with non-relevant information they might feel what kind of impact could they make anyhow.

Do we truly see each other or has our perspective been manipulated rather than elevated? Communication technology is not only helping to divide us, it is also not utilizing our capabilities and interests to their full potential, slapping a layer of technology on antiquated Madison Avenue Ad models and top-heavy worker models defining who we should be to serve the market rather than what we could become to better serve ourselves to the serve the market purposefully.

If you believe I am over-generalizing, what percentage of advertisements through the connection speaks to the core of your interests and situations? What percentage of the experiences you find on the web speak to the core of who you are or who you want to become? Is the web helping paint your own picture or is it painting the picture for you? Now if you do feel the web speaks to you as you have the skills to master it, what about others? How is the connection serving society as a whole?

And that is exactly what this podcast is about however long it lasts. An ongoing dialogue on how communication technology could bring more people into what is possible within the human condition. Asking the question, what is possible when we are connected and in control? Moving forward this is the question I want to pose on this podcast to the brightest minds regardless of their income level, occupation, gender, age, religion, or race.

To reach deep into all corners of society reaching past what is expected from us to what is possible through the lens of communication technology. I don't care if it is a fortune 500 CEO or a high schooler from Harlem, what could be built to help tap into human potential to bring more of us into a better future. Not a perfect future. A better future. Who doesn't want that?

What tools and methodologies are being built to accomplish this? Who are the people building these tools? How can they be helped to accomplish their missions? What are the barriers standing in the way? How can these barriers be removed?

And let me be clear, technology is not a panacea for all of our ills. It is a tool. If we want to move a boulder, we can either blow it up or make a lever. I argue for the latter. To me, this is the Emergence. This is the movement to build tools to reach into our potential.

The emergence is for social impact investors who want to build technology to empower consumers with choice, employers who see their employees beyond only a conduit for revenue, civic innovators, and politicians who see technology as a catalyst for social progress without sacrificing the innovative spirit of the markets, technologists who want to build a more resonant connection, and most importantly people of all stripes who believe we can do better than this.

Do we want a healthy society, where everyone has a seat at the table of life, liberty, and the pursuit of happiness? Something written in the American Declaration of Independence yet an incredibly universal ideal. An ideal that anyone in the political spectrum would agree with unless it was tyrannical in nature, I would imagine.

The theme of this episode and hopefully many to come is how technology and systems of thought provide the tools for all members of society to play an active role in its overall health. To increase creativity, awareness, productivity, and empathy amongst all people. To create a baseline for a quality of life based not only on the will of the people or the promises of their politicians but through an exchange of value between people, business, and government. When have the people ever had the chance to put their hands on the lever to balance all three? The flow of information is one of the most powerful levers people have at their disposal. I am convinced when they are allowed to put their hands on it they will do amazing things.

Democracies are never guaranteed. In their natural evolution, through the threads of representation, the strong always rise to lead. When this strength blames weakness over understanding as a means of control, a vacuum is created where extremes thrive. At least this is the way I see it. Democracies have never had the toolset we have at our disposal to balance strength with understanding, where opportunity favors both the weak and the strong.

I have noticed over the years, the internet has grown into a framework more to identify problems rather than to work on solutions. It is understandable as problems are a lot easier to digest than solutions. Believe me, I will be the first to admit there are wonderful solutions coming from the connection, but as a whole, it seems to amplify reaction over inquiry trading more in the binaries of agreement and disagreement rather than collaboration and deep engagement.

In Conclusion

I personally believe in God and believe the reason we are here is to exercise our true potential to improve ourselves and the communities we interact with. Maybe the reason the world is full of challenges is for us to adapt and overcome while we are here. To evolve into better representations of self and how we contribute to the whole. I don't believe we have ever had the toolset to accomplish this as tools have always favored systems over individuals but this reality may be changing with new frameworks and tools to harness what lies within these systems which are the people.

Whether one believes in God, energy, or science as the reason for our existence, purpose is what could move all of us forward. Purpose not architected for us but by us. Purpose extended beyond the strong and resilient to the unfortunate, the marginalized, and the lost souls. History has proven controls over purpose favors unequal distribution of power and influence "for the people". Moving these controls "with the people" could help move us into parity with systems of business and government. Maybe this all sounds like a pipe dream or fanciful thinking but I see it as a plan.

A plan to help identify and create awareness around frameworks, legislation, AI, and applications to build a purpose-driven future. Technology is not the savior here. It is not a replacement for social programs or philanthropic endeavors. It is a lever to help bring more people into systems of governance, business and social engagement to both help themselves and to build systems more representative of the interests of all people. It is less about how bad the connection is and more about how good it could become.

This is the quest of The Emergence. To explore and uncover what and who is out there to drive these better realities forward. It could be a business leader, technologist, politician, scientist, teacher, student, worker, social worker, or somebody out on the street. I don't have many answers but I have questions I believe might help strengthen our core to inspire better systems with these better systems strengthening the core of society. A purposeful feedback loop that over time could lead to better realities.

So join me on this quest called The Emergence at the podcast site theemergence.io and on Youtube where in future episodes I will unpack these ideas through essays, commentary, and dialogs with intellectually curious people to surface technologies and methodologies to help move the human condition forward.

I ask if you find these ideas interesting and important at least as a kernel of an idea to help build a better connection that you share this podcast and future episodes with those you feel this may resonate with. I have also created a free ebook and a paperback available on Amazon for purchase on this intro episode and have broken the intro down into sections linked to within this episode on Youtube to make it easier to share relatable topics with others.

I am always interested in finding interesting people to have conversations with around these ideas so feel free to email me at theemergenceio@gmail.com if you know of someone who would like to engage around the ideas behind The Emergence.

Bibliography

College Tuition Costs Soar Chart of the Day – Bloomberg News
bloomberg.com/news/articles/2014-08-18/college-tuition-costs-soar-chart-of-the-day

New Legislation in U.S. proposes federal data protection agency – CPO Magazine
cpomagazine.com/data-protection/new-legislation-in-u-s-proposes-federal-data-protection-agency-broad-range-of-new-enforcement-actions/?mc_cid=d3309c3698

1033 program to transfer military arms to local police departments – Wikipedia

en.wikipedia.org/wiki/Law_Enforcement_Support_Office#:~:te
xt=Section%201033%20of%20the%20National.and%20count
er%2Dterrorism%20activities%22.

Since 2015, 20 states have made Mental Health First Aid a
priority by enacting policies that allocate funding for trainings
mentalhealthfirstaid.org/about/advocacy

U.S. Suicide Rate Climbed 35% in two decades – US News
usnews.com/news/health-news/articles/2020-04-08/us-suicide
-rate-climbed-35-37-in-two-decades

Hitler Radio – Transdiffusion.org
transdiffusion.org/2008/01/07/hitlers_radio

Rwandan Genocide – Wikipedia
en.wikipedia.org/wiki/Radio_Télévision_Libre_des_Mille_Colli
nes

William Randolph Hearst Manufacturing Stories – Stanford
web.stanford.edu/class/e297a/Impact%20Media%20has%20
During%20War.htm

Watch this Essay on Youtube
youtube.com/watch?v=uaVY6zlfYNQ&t=4s

Listen to this Essay on Substack
theemergence1.substack.com/p/introduction-to-the-emergenc
e-466#details

Chapter 14
Technology, Direct Democracy, And Lost Potential Of A Truly
Engaged Electorate
Originally Published 11/5/20

Welcome to the Emergence, a podcast asking the question,
what is possible when we are connected and in control? My
name is J. Paul Duplantis and today's episode will focus on
the idea of technology helping give voice to the electorate. A
concept of Direct Democracy experimented with for
thousands of years yet never fully realized. What is different
today is the technology at our disposal to close the gap
between the will of the people and actions from the
government. Technology to move influence past a reliance on
lobbyists, interest groups, and bureaucratic maneuvering.

Civic technologies have existed for years to increase civic
engagement but only through a patchwork of applications. In
the eyes of the Emergence, what is needed is more of a
universal framework to securely connect the electorate with
what is being drafted in the name of the people. A framework
to balance the interests of people, business, and government
through the sharing of feedback and ideas from the electorate
into systems of governance.

One potential framework on the horizon I believe speaks well
to this is the Solid Framework, led by the founder of the web,
Tim Berners Lee. In March of 2020, I had reached out to
members of the Solid team who had drafted a study on
engaging the citizenry of Flanders, Belgium with municipal
services securely and directly through Solid Personal Online
Datastores or what they call Solid PODS. I asked Raf Buyle
who is a co-author of the study if he believed the technology
could be extended to potentially allow citizens to engage with

legislation directly, serving as a vehicle for direct democracy. He mentioned in his reply he did feel it was possible which I will cover in a moment.

It is important to note that at the end of September 2020, the Solid team announced they are now implementing this technology throughout the city of Flanders to allow the citizenry to engage with municipal services securely through Solid PODS. Could this be a first step toward a path of technology framework empowering Direct Democracy? Only time will tell.

But before I read the essay detailing the technology behind this potential empowerment of the electorate and Raf Buyle's reply, I would like to provide more of a setup outside the scope of the technology to why I believe the fundamentals of an engaged electorate are important for democracies to thrive. I recently learned of something through a deep dive into the rabbit hole of those critical of the UN's Agenda 21 to promote global sustainability which I feel might help provide more context.

I will stay neutral on my thoughts on Agenda 21 other than the fact I argue for a clean planet and opportunities and justice for all. But I do realize the path to progress can be littered with consequences whether intended or not.

What I learned from the critiques of Agenda 21 is the concern of non-elected officials infiltrating local governments through something called a Delphi technique which is a method of group decision-making and forecasting through the judgments of experts influencing legislation. Even though I do see the conspiratorial nature of the Delphi technique being used as a proxy for the U.N. to eventually depopulate rural areas, the notion of using non elected experts to influence legislation resonated with me and I felt served as an effective lens to see the ideas of direct democracy through.

Is it too hard to believe there could be a global agenda to push standards for communities all over the world to follow to end in a more sustainable future for mother earth? Personally, I don't see this as nefarious by nature as I wish for a much cleaner planet but how would these standards impact the labor market, the housing market, and the market in general in our communities regardless of where we live in the world?

Are they in the true interest of the people who live in these communities or are they in the interest of the politicians, the contractors, and the institutions who have an ideological or financial stake in the success of the programs resulting from the agenda? Or just as important, the same could be said for those fighting the pursuit of sustainability. Do they have the true interest of the people at heart or are they looking to protect their own business interests over that of the communities that surround them. How would we know when we are not involved?

I also believe there is an agenda to limit competition between information carriers and big tech impacting the affordability, accessibility, and quality of the flow of information to end users. Do the end products of Cox communications, Google, Twitter or Facebook behind the flow of information have the true interest of the people at heart? Or do they serve the interests of their shareholders, the politicians, and other organizations who have an ideological or financial stake in the success of the programs resulting from their agenda.

When the net worth of these companies become larger than the GDP of many countries on earth, what are the chances the information they deliver would serve the bottom line of anyone else other than themselves? Is all of humanity at the service of a bottom line and do we want more of a stake in determining the bottom line are the questions to ask.

I chose the two agendas above as examples to consider as I believe one speaks to the potential of a healthier planet and the other speaks to the potential of healthier minds inhabiting the planet. Two agendas incredibly important to the health of society in general, but when outside the reach of the people, are muted in their full potential. Potential robbed by dissonance coursing through the electorate drowned out by the illusion of representation.

How prominent is the Delphi technique in politics? Where lobbyists, associations, and NGAs use money and political capital to influence legislation locally and nationally to put forth agendas favorable to all corners of the political spectrum. To use influence to seize private property, bypass environmental standards, or push through tax loopholes to name a few.

I would imagine it would be impossible to quantify but it does beg the question when people are not actively involved with their governance, how influential could they really be in their governing? When they are not involved, what business and/or institutional interests are filling this void? Are the legislative proxies of their politicians enough to overcome these forces to build a truly representative government?

Clearly, what exists today favors the building of systems of governance and commerce to optimize societal outcomes but shouldn't the people have more of a voice in building these systems? Shouldn't outcomes be more reflective of those it is built to serve? I know the argument too well that people should not be trusted to participate at a level beyond voting for their representatives. Or that people have better things to do than to be involved civically at such a level. Or that nothing would ever get done with too many cooks in the kitchen.

I actually shared an email with the founder of Govtrack.us on this very topic where he mentioned this style of technology has been tried countless times to no avail and people have better things to do with their time. Under the current framework, he might be correct, whereas if what we see from the greater web was copy and pasted into civic engagement down to the legislative level, there is a high probability people would be wasting their time as the noise would be deafening.

But there are technologies on the horizon to change the very fabric of the web from a system driven by providers to one driven by people and the Solid Framework is at the front of this push. What would be possible if technology securely aligned the interests and situations of people with legislation and those who crafted it?

Not to match every piece of legislation with every person impacted but to match topics within legislation and procedures being drafted with those highly interested and engaged in the topic. Not only feedback and ideas cultivated from experts and providers in related fields but stakeholders in the communities served. Feedback and ideas not to replace the efforts of experts and politicians but to inform their positions organically from deep within the system of governance.

Feedback and ideas on cancer research funding coming from a physician's assistant for an oncologist. On education reform from a teacher or parent who homeschools their child. On a highway expansion through a community from the commuters and homeowners in the area. What could a framework built for stakeholder interests to resonate into laws passed on their behalf do to build a more representative government and society in general?

This is the purpose of this episode which is to inspire thought and awareness around these ideas and future episodes to engage technologists, government officials, and community members around what might be possible when technology aligns the governed with the governing more effectively.

Yes, we can vote for a council member representing our community but what percentage of people who vote really understand how the person will represent their interests? And what are the chances, what the candidate promises aligns with what the candidate fights for? Not to say we should not vote for the candidate but I have to wonder if our vote is muted when we are not heard at the process level. Maybe when we are more in tune with the processes of governing, we may finally get to a point where we will begin to demand better choices for representation as well as learn to more effectively sniff out games played by institutions to influence elections or bypass legislation.

The root word of democracy is from the greek word demos meaning a whole citizen living within a particular city-state. Are we anywhere close to being whole in how we are represented? I believe technology reaching deep within the electorate to inform and hold representation accountable could help move us toward a more resonant form of democracy where we are more fully represented.

Chapter 15
A Conversation on Solid PODS and Direct Democracy
Originally Published 3/6/2020

I recently ran across a study and use case

ruben.verborgh.org/publications/buyle_egose_2019/

on using Personalized Online Data Stores (PODS) to help the citizens of Flanders, Belgium communicate more effectively with their representative government. Having followed the progress of Solid PODS over the last couple of years and an advocate for decentralizing the web and applications serving the web, I had reached out to the team to see how their technology may one day allow citizens to securely engage with legislation directly.

Direct Democracy is not a new concept and has been experimented with since Athenian democracy in the 5th century BC en.m.wikipedia.org/wiki/Direct_democracy but the represented have never had the toolset to engage with the inner workings of government in real-time regardless of their location until now. Yet even though the technology is currently possible; the network, AI layer, and application layer remain a toolset outside of user control compromising the relationship between user data and government data. But recently a major push to decentralize this toolset by companies such as Inrupt with their Solid POD framework and Singularitynet's decentralized AI framework will begin to move controls over to the user.

As this becomes a reality, what is possible when these tools are used to provide people a pathway to their government not only through their representatives but through the policies and legislation crafted on their behalf. We might be amazed by what may surface from an electorate engaged beyond the promises of their representatives. As there are many flavors of Direct Democracy, this essay intends to elevate awareness and feedback on legislation as it is drafted. Extending this to the actual vote outside of local levels has the potential to invite a tyranny of the majority to legislate, so there are caveats beyond tech to consider.

But what is the downside to bringing more of the electorate into the process of governing to help see behind the curtain of the cult of personality? To attach their interests to policy ultimately affecting their lives and their communities. Is an involved electorate healthy for society? How could it not be?

As one can see in the email exchange I will read next, the technology and the talent is upon us. Now, what do we do with our role in government? Do we participate in it or do we anticipate what is drafted for us by it? Thomas Jefferson once said, "I know of no safe depository of the ultimate powers of the society but the people themselves; and if we think them not enlightened enough to exercise their control with a wholesome discretion, the remedy is not to take it from them, but inform their discretion." Which leads me to wonder what the enlightenment thinkers of the day would have rendered with this toolset at their disposal?

My email to the team....

I'm very interested in this paper you have collaborated on where Solid PODS are used for government applications. I had written an essay titled Emergent Representation of the People where I argue for the ability of the electorate to interact directly with legislation as it is drafted.

As I read through your paper, I am wondering if legislation could be drafted in a POD with each Committee Member involved having their own POD and a commenter with their POD attaching feedback to passages attached to the source material. I would envision the legislators being able to turn on layers of commentary and vote up the contributions best speaking to the passages in question. I would also envision some type of citation or badge that would sit in the commentator's POD to remind the electorate of their contributions.

Does this sound possible? Or more importantly, practical?

Curious to hear your thoughts.

Reply from Raf Buyle

Dear Paul,

It might be a good idea to facilitate the drafting process of legislation using multiple PODs.

In the region of Flanders in Belgium, almost all departments, agencies and cabinets take part in the preparation of legislation of the Flemish Government. Both before and during the formal decision-making procedure, many institutions and organisations are involved to give feedback on the proposals for decisions and decrees. The decision-making process in the Flemish Government itself usually goes through several formal approval steps. After final approval by the government, decrees go to Parliament. All regulations are translated and published in the Belgian Official Gazette. Finally, they are integrated into the Codex — which is now available as linked open data — and published on the Web.

The process of requesting and issuing advice, budget verification, related decisions, decrees, laws, guidelines, and coordinated legal texts, is supported by various specialised information systems. Thanks to better coordination, the exchange between the different actors could be streamlined with less need for manual verifications of versions of documents. By applying a decentralised architecture based on Solid to the drafting process of legislation, we could raise the transparency of the decision-making process. By applying the principles of linked data — linking the coined semantics to existing vocabularies — legislation would become more 'harmonised' and 'digital friendly', which raises legal interoperability.

The regional Government of Flanders facilitates a more transparent local decision-making process by publishing local council decisions as Linked Open Data. This initiative — started in 2015 — created an Open Source editor, which supports administrations to write and publish linked decisions without additional efforts. A vibrant community of administrations, companies and academia are involved in the development of the software.

Given the opportunity of streamlining the processes of the different stakeholders involved in drafting and reviewing legislation, the opportunity to involve the citizen and the potential increase in provenance and transparenty, we think it's valuable to combine the good practices of the 'Linked Legislation Editor' with the strengths of Solid.

That is the end of the email reply. I have included the link to the Solid Pod study in the podcast notes. Thank you for listening to today's episode. I hope to find interesting people to bring on the show in the future to dig deeper into the potential of technology and direct democracy.

The paper on Linked Legislation (early start of the project, now in production):
biblio.ugent.be/publication/8557584/file/855758

Chapter 16
We Have A Communication Problem
Originally Published 5/7/22

WE HAVE A COMMUNICATION PROBLEM. An essay by J. Paul Duplantis

Google controls 92% of online searches.

Amazon controls $41% of online shopping.

Facebook controls 71% of social online visits in the U.S.

(Stats from Statista.com)

We have a communication problem.

A problem I believe not for profit funding, open source software development, and community involvement can help fix.

What is the problem?

We are influenced by what we read, watch, and listen to which in turn influences what we say, what we believe, and how we act. Look around and look inside. Sometimes it is subtle. Sometimes not so much.

Currently billion dollar and trillion dollar companies have the keys to this influence through algorithms, databases, and query tools they exclusively control. This influence is amplified by algorithms tuned to the interests of advertising and subscription models attached to shareholder value with user attention serving as collateral for future Investments. Do you want your attention to be collateral for investment groups or short sellers? I know I don't.

So every time we login to an information silo created for profit, we are pledging the experiences we create, consume, or share to the interests of organizations whose sole mission is perpetual growth realized through these profits. Watch the movie Executive Suite with William Holden from 1954. The producers of that movie knew what was coming.

Of course profits are necessary to drive innovation and employment but should they be the drivers of what we say or what we think? Historically communication technology had more of a passive role in influencing our behaviors as there was more of a separation between our behaviors and the interests of providers.

Ma Bell didn't know what you were making for dinner now did she.

But this line has all but been removed allowing providers an unprecedented level of control over perception and relevance of what is discovered, created, shared, and commented on. This is leading to an ultimate feedback loop optimized to drive profits more than the capabilities and interests of people.

How can this problem be fixed? By harnessing not for profit funding, open source technologies, and community engagement to begin to shift priorities toward the quality of the user experience rather than the quantity of it.

To

increase a thirst for knowledge across a wider swath
of people
verify the authenticity of content found
inspire collaboration across platforms and silos of
information

To

protect user data
provide people more choice in how we discover
information, goods, and services
and improve the quality of communication between
people, business, and government

I mean big money is donated to good causes without
expectation of profit every day, why should exploring the
highest common denominator in how we communicate be any
less important?

To be clear, I am not saying to demonetize what content,
goods or services are discovered but how they are
discovered. We now have the infrastructure built to engage
half the world. Should the overall arc of the engagement be
for the private good or the public good is the question. I argue
there is a social cost and opportunity cost for the majority of
people connected when how we communicate is prioritized for
the wealth of the few over the physical, mental, and emotional
health of the many.

Look around at the pervasiveness of homelessness, drug
addiction, suicides, and extreme views of people.

Look at the rising cost of living to include higher education, housing, food, and healthcare in relation to the availability of roles to support these increases.

Look at the misalignment of competencies between services and support in business, between those in need and the resources to help, and between the capabilities of labor and the demands of employers.

What role does the communication problem play in all of this? I am not certain but it is adding noise to what we are discovering and amplifying problems rather than solving them? I am not placing all of societal ills at the feet of communication technology but I believe there is a fundamental responsibility of those building these tools to help tap into the potential and purpose of people.

Think about it for a minute. If more people found purpose in what they did and those efforts were validated and rewarded more often, wouldn't this help reduce social costs? Don't these costs affect us all in one way or another?

The good news is there are a number of platforms and methodologies coming online to help free people from the influence of centralized providers over the information they create, consume, and share. From Tim Berners Lee's solid framework to the decentralized database of Gun DB to Blockchain technology, there are a vast amount of resources here today and on the horizon to help put people in the driver seat of their experiences.

But the communication problem is not just about the failings of technology but how technology should be learning more from the best aspects of human nature to fold back into the application of the technology. I mean how many stories are out there during times of tragedy where people come together to help one another? What triggers this spirit in humans and how could technology tap into this?

This is the cycle that needs to be visited to build a web as well as virtual and augmented worlds to better represent the potential of people these technologies should serve. To create a partnership between not for profit funders, technologists, and communities to build out databases, query structures, and algorithms to empower discovery and sharing without compromising user data or manipulating outcomes.

Imagine the creation of a query tool to help a customer identify a support person within an organization best suited to address their problem as well as identify resources highly relevant to their issue. Now imagine this tool could be embedded into other organizations free of charge and be improved upon by the open source development community, all while keeping the company data secure.

Imagine introducing this model into the policing community to help open channels of communication between community members and those who are sworn to protect and serve. Or to more effectively align the interests of homeless advocates with the needs of the homeless.

Or to create a dating site independent of centralized control where the experiences could be moved to another site with a different query algorithm without sacrificing the relationships people have already built. Or to create a movie network built around matching themes and words found within movies with what resonates with the moviegoer the most at the moment of discovery.

Now imagine all of the examples listed above not requiring a login to experience, not harvesting user data for the benefit of the application or third parties, and not requiring a subscription to access. Then imagine having at your disposal a variety of ways to pay for the content found to include micropayments for sections of content, task based rewarding, crypto, gifting, or ads based entirely on user choice.

Let me ask you. Are you OK with the current model built to serve you information, news, entertainment and relationships. Don't you want less friction and controls over what you are discovering? Don't you want more choices?

All of the solutions I have described are possible but how feasible are they to scale under a for profit model, especially considering none of the underlying code or the resulting experiences would ever be exclusive to a provider. Could these solutions exist within a for profit motive? Maybe, but all I see is more of the same on the horizon while the problems will become less apparent as we continue to be fed convenience over clarity.

Hey, I admit I fall victim to this all the time whether it is a product delivered the same day by Amazon or a video found for home repair on YouTube but I wonder what would be possible if my attention wasn't only optimized for a price. And this is the mission of The Emergence which is to uncover communities, technologies, methodologies, talent, use cases, and financial resources that speak to this new model to increase the quality of communication by limiting the influence of money and power over it.

Moving forward, I plan on digging deep to find where these solutions would best serve people, businesses, and government and bring these stories to the podcast to serve as challenges for innovators in technology, finance, and community development to tackle. I will also dig to find what is already built, what could be modified or what could be created from scratch to meet these challenges to bring to the attention of not for profit funders. These challenges will be made available on TheEmergence.io with links to Github repositories of code identified as relevant to the challenge serving as a gateway for philanthropists to consider for funding.

The question here is what could be done to harness technology to engage people at the very core of what they can bring to themselves and to society in general.

Ask yourself if you feel this is important. If it is, let's do something about it.

Watch this essay on Youtube
youtube.com/watch?v=M78dAio2Glo

Listen to this Essay on Substack
theemergence1.substack.com/p/we-have-a-communication-problem-8b9

AUDIO PODCASTS

The following are Episodes recorded for TheEmergence podcast. Oldest to Newest

Link to the Podcast.

On Substack
theemergence1.substack.com/

On Youtube
youtube.com/@theemergencepodcast6292

Episode 1
Introduction to the Emergence
theemergence1.substack.com/p/introduction-to-the-emergenc e-466#details

Episode 2
Awareness & Context
theemergence1.substack.com/p/awareness-and-context-b77# details

Episode 3
Time to Clean Up The American Presidential Debates
theemergence1.substack.com/p/time-to-clean-up-the-america
n-presidential-738

Episode 4
The Future of Work
theemergence1.substack.com/p/the-future-of-work-15e

Episode 5
Technology, Direct Democracy, And Lost Potential Of A Truly
Engaged Electorate
theemergence1.substack.com/p/technology-direct-democracy
-and-lost-295

Episode 6
Exploring Human Potential
theemergence1.substack.com/p/exploring-human-potential-13
6

Episode 7
A Conversation With Cybernetician Javier Livas Cantu
theemergence1.substack.com/p/a-conversation-with-cyberneti
cian-eac

Episode 8
Building A Better Future Through A Decentralized Connection
With GunDB Founder Mark Nadal
theemergence1.substack.com/p/building-a-better-future-throu
gh-567

Episode 9
Exploring The Connection And Human Potential With Tim McLain
theemergence1.substack.com/p/exploring-the-connection-and-human-005

Episode 10
Building Trust And Community On The Web With Sebastiaan van der Lans
theemergence1.substack.com/p/building-trust-and-community-on-the-fdd

Episode 11
Exploring The Potential Of Connected Communities
theemergence1.substack.com/p/exploring-the-potential-of-connected-323

Episode 12
The Emergent Web
theemergence1.substack.com/p/the-emergent-web-70c

Episode 13
Free Market Parity Through Decentralization
theemergence1.substack.com/p/free-market-parity-through-decentralization-306

Episode 14
The Emergence Mission
theemergence1.substack.com/p/the-emergence-mission-e3a

Episode 15
Common Sense By Thomas Paine
theemergence1.substack.com/p/common-sense-by-thomas-paine-557

Episode 16
Homelessness, Technology, Awareness, And Understanding
theemergence1.substack.com/p/homelessness-technology-a
wareness-be3

Episode 17
The Tunable Web
theemergence1.substack.com/p/the-tunable-web-1af

Episode 18
Awakening The Soul Of Power - A Conversation With Author
Christian de la Huerta
theemergence1.substack.com/p/awakening-the-soul-of-power
-a-conversation-7d6

Episode 19
The Information Trap
theemergence1.substack.com/p/the-information-trap-544

Episode 20
Augmented And Virtual Reality With Rami Kalla From Point In
Time Studios
theemergence1.substack.com/p/augmented-and-virtual-reality
-with-c0b

Episode 21
Why Discovery Should Not Be Exclusive To Distribution
theemergence1.substack.com/p/augmented-and-virtual-reality
-with-c0b

Episode 22
Exploring The Value Of Labor With Carlos Castro
theemergence1.substack.com/p/exploring-the-value-of-labor-
with-829

Episode 23
Discussing Worker Co-Ops With ASU Post Doctoral Associate
Nigel Forrest
/theemergence1.substack.com/p/discussing-worker-co-ops-wi
th-asu-553

Episode 24
Communication Breakdown And The Marginalized Consumer
theemergence1.substack.com/p/communication-breakdown-a
nd-the-marginalized-364

Episode 25
We Have A Communication Problem
theemergence1.substack.com/p/we-have-a-communication-pr
oblem-8b9